ALASKA TRAVEL GUIDE 2023/2024

The Updated Guide to Planning Your Trip to Alaska. Tips and Practical Information. Uncovers Everything You Need to Know to Plan A Trip.

Travel Adventurer

Copyrighted Material

All rights reserved. No part of this publication may be reproduced, distributed, or transmitted in any form or by any means, including photocopying, recording, or other electronic or mechanical methods, without the prior written permission of the publisher, except in the case of brief quotations embodied in critical reviews and certain other noncommercial uses permitted by copyright law.

This publication is intended for informational purposes only and does not constitute professional advice. The author and publisher have made every effort to ensure the accuracy of the information herein, but cannot be held responsible for any errors, omissions, or damages arising from the use of this information.

All trademarks, logos, and images used in this publication are the property of their respective owners. Any unauthorized use or reproduction is strictly prohibited.

Copyright©2023 Travel Adventurer

All Rights Reserved

Table of Contents

My Alaska Travel Experience	6
CHAPTER 1	**10**
Introduction	**10**
Why Visit Alaska?	10
Purpose of the Guide	14
CHAPTER 2	**18**
Understanding Alaska	**18**
Geography and Climate	18
Wildlife and Natural Wonders	21
Cultural Diversity	24
CHAPTER 3	**28**
When to Go	**28**
Best Time to Visit Alaska	28
Seasonal Considerations	31
CHAPTER 4	**36**
Planning Your Itinerary	**36**
Duration of Stay	36

Choosing Destinations	38
Transportation Options	42
CHAPTER 5	**48**
Accommodation Options	**48**
Hotels and Resorts	48
Lodges and Cabins	51
Camping and RV Parks	54
CHAPTER 6	**58**
Getting There	**58**
Air Travel to Alaska	58
Cruising to Alaska	62
Driving to Alaska	66
CHAPTER 7	**72**
Visa and Entry Requirements	**72**
Passport Requirements	72
Visa Regulations	76
CHAPTER 8	**78**
Health and Safety Tips	**78**
Vaccinations and Medical Preparations	78

Wildlife Safety Guidelines	82
Emergency Services	86
CHAPTER 9	**90**
Packing Essentials	**90**
Clothing and Gear Recommendations	90
Essential Documents and Money	93
CHAPTER 10	**100**
Activities and Attractions	**100**
Outdoor Adventures (hiking, fishing, kayaking, etc.)	100
Wildlife Viewing Opportunities	104
Cultural Experiences (museums, festivals, etc.)	108
CHAPTER 11	**112**
Food and Dining Options	**112**
Local Cuisine and Seafood Specialties	112
Dining Recommendations	115
CHAPTER 12	**118**
Budgeting and Expenses	**118**
Cost Considerations for Alaska Travel	118
Money-Saving Tips	122

CHAPTER 13	**128**
Communication and Connectivity	**128**
Mobile Networks and Internet Access	128
Communication Tips for Remote Areas	131
CHAPTER 14	**136**
Travel Insurance	**136**
Importance of Travel Insurance	136
Coverage Options	138
CHAPTER 15	**142**
Responsible Travel Practices	**142**
Environmental Conservation	142
Respect for Local Communities	144
CHAPTERT 16	**148**
Conclusion	**148**

My Alaska Travel Experience

On a certain day, my dear friend, I embarked on an unforgettable journey to the breathtaking land of Alaska. It was a place where nature's magnificence danced with the human spirit, leaving an indelible mark on my heart. Allow me to share with you the captivating story of my visit, filled with emotions that still stir within me.

As I stepped off the plane, a rush of crisp, invigorating air greeted me like an old friend. The scent of pine trees and the distant sound of rushing water whispered promises of adventure and discovery. I couldn't help but feel a sense of awe as I gazed upon the vast expanse of untouched wilderness stretching out before me.

My first stop was Denali National Park, home to the majestic Denali, North America's tallest peak. The mountain stood tall and proud, its snow-capped summit piercing through the clouds like a beacon of grandeur. I joined a group of fellow adventurers on a hike through the park, our footsteps echoing in harmony with nature's symphony.

As we trekked deeper into the wilderness, our guide regaled us with tales of survival and resilience. He spoke of how the animals adapted to the harsh winters, their fur coats acting as shields against the biting cold. We encountered a family of caribou grazing peacefully in a meadow, their antlers reaching towards the sky like intricate works of art. It was a humbling sight, reminding me of the delicate balance between man and nature.

One evening, we gathered around a crackling campfire under a star-studded sky. The Northern Lights danced above us, painting the heavens with vibrant hues of green and purple. It was as if nature itself had become an artist, creating a masterpiece for our eyes only. In that moment, I felt connected to something greater than myself – a sense of wonder that transcended words.

Continuing my journey, I found myself in the charming town of Juneau, nestled between towering mountains and the sparkling waters of the Inside Passage. I embarked on a whale-watching excursion, hoping to catch a glimpse of these gentle giants in their natural habitat. As if on cue, a humpback whale breached the surface, its massive body soaring into the air before gracefully diving back into the depths. It was a sight that left me breathless, reminding me of the sheer power and beauty that resides within our oceans.

In Anchorage, I had the privilege of meeting a group of indigenous people who shared their ancestral wisdom with me. They spoke of their deep connection to the land and their efforts to preserve their cultural heritage. Their stories painted a vivid picture of resilience and determination, reminding me of the importance of honoring our roots and protecting our planet.

As my time in Alaska drew to a close, I couldn't help but feel a bittersweet longing in my heart. The memories I had made, the sights I had seen, and the emotions I had experienced would forever be etched in my soul. Alaska had taught me to appreciate the raw beauty of nature, to embrace adventure with an open heart, and to cherish every moment as if it were my last.

CHAPTER 1

Introduction

Why Visit Alaska?

Alaska, the largest state in the United States, offers a unique and unparalleled experience for travelers. From its stunning natural landscapes to its rich cultural heritage, Alaska has something to offer for everyone. Here are several reasons why visiting Alaska should be on your travel bucket list:

Breathtaking Natural Beauty: Alaska is renowned for its breathtaking natural beauty, which includes towering mountains, vast glaciers, pristine lakes, and abundant wildlife. The state is home to numerous national parks and protected areas, such as Denali National Park and Preserve, Glacier Bay National Park and Preserve, and Kenai Fjords National Park. These areas provide visitors with the opportunity to witness awe-inspiring landscapes and observe diverse wildlife in their natural habitats. Whether it's hiking through rugged terrains, kayaking among icebergs, or spotting grizzly bears and bald eagles, Alaska's natural beauty never fails to leave a lasting impression.

Unique Outdoor Activities: Alaska offers a wide range of outdoor activities that cater to adventure enthusiasts and nature lovers alike. Fishing enthusiasts can enjoy world-class salmon fishing in the state's rivers and streams, while thrill-seekers can embark on exhilarating whitewater rafting trips. The state is also a haven for hikers, with countless trails offering varying levels of difficulty and stunning views. Additionally, visitors can partake in activities such as dog sledding, glacier trekking, heli-skiing, and even witnessing the mesmerizing Northern Lights during winter months. These unique outdoor experiences allow travelers to immerse themselves in Alaska's rugged wilderness and create unforgettable memories.

Rich Cultural Heritage: Alaska is home to a diverse array of indigenous cultures that have thrived in the region for thousands of years. Exploring Alaska provides an opportunity to learn about these vibrant cultures through visits to museums, cultural centers, and interactions with local communities. Native Alaskan art, music, dance performances, and traditional crafts offer a glimpse into the rich heritage of the state. Additionally, attending cultural events and festivals, such as the Alaska Native Heritage Center's Gathering of Native Artists or the World Eskimo-Indian Olympics, allows visitors to witness and appreciate the traditions and customs that have shaped Alaska's cultural identity.

Abundance of Wildlife: Alaska is renowned for its abundant wildlife, making it a paradise for nature enthusiasts and wildlife photographers. The state is home to a diverse range of species, including brown bears, moose, caribou, wolves, whales, sea lions, and numerous bird species. Visitors can embark on wildlife viewing tours or take a cruise along the coastline to witness these magnificent creatures in their natural habitats. The coastal waters of Alaska are particularly famous for their whale-watching opportunities, with humpback whales and orcas being commonly sighted. Observing these majestic animals up close is an experience that leaves a lasting impression on visitors.

Unspoiled Wilderness: Alaska boasts vast expanses of unspoiled wilderness that remain largely untouched by human development. The state's remote locations offer a sense of solitude and tranquility that is increasingly rare in today's world. Whether it's exploring the vast tundra of the Arctic National Wildlife Refuge or cruising through the Inside Passage's fjords, visitors can escape the hustle and bustle of everyday life and reconnect with nature in its purest form. The pristine landscapes of Alaska provide a sense of awe and wonder that is unparalleled.

Outdoor Photography Opportunities: For photography enthusiasts, Alaska presents endless opportunities to capture stunning images. From capturing the vibrant colors of fall foliage to photographing glaciers calving into the ocean, every corner of Alaska offers a unique subject for photographers. The state's dramatic landscapes, wildlife encounters, and ever-changing weather conditions provide an ideal setting for capturing breathtaking shots. Whether you are an amateur photographer or a seasoned professional, Alaska's natural beauty will inspire and challenge your skills.

Culinary Delights: Alaska's culinary scene is as diverse as its landscapes. The state's pristine waters provide an abundance of fresh seafood, including salmon, halibut, and king crab, which are staples of Alaskan cuisine. Visitors can indulge in a wide range of seafood dishes, from freshly caught fish grilled to perfection to succulent crab legs. Additionally, Alaska's wild game, such as moose and reindeer, offers a unique dining experience for those seeking to explore the local flavors. The state also boasts a growing craft beer and distillery scene, with breweries and distilleries offering tastings and tours.

Rich History: Alaska has a rich history that dates back thousands of years. From the indigenous peoples who have inhabited the region for millennia to the gold rush era that brought thousands of prospectors to the state in the late 19th century, Alaska's history is filled with fascinating stories and events. Visitors can explore historical sites such as Skagway's Klondike Gold Rush National Historical Park or visit museums like the Anchorage Museum to learn about Alaska's past. Understanding the history of the state adds depth and context to the overall travel experience.

In conclusion, visiting Alaska offers an once-in-a-lifetime opportunity to immerse oneself in breathtaking natural beauty, engage in unique outdoor activities, learn about diverse cultures, witness abundant wildlife, and experience unspoiled wilderness. Whether you are seeking adventure, tranquility, cultural enrichment, or simply a chance to disconnect from the modern world, Alaska has it all.

Purpose of the Guide

The purpose of the guide "Planning Your Trip to Alaska: Tips and Practical Information" is to provide comprehensive and practical guidance for individuals who are planning a trip to Alaska. This guide aims to assist travelers in making informed decisions and ensuring a smooth and enjoyable experience during their visit to this unique and breathtaking destination.

One of the primary purposes of this guide is to offer tips and advice on various aspects of planning a trip to Alaska. It covers essential topics such as when to visit, how to get there, transportation options within the state, accommodation choices, popular attractions and activities, safety considerations, and budgeting tips. By providing this information, the guide helps travelers make well-informed decisions based on their preferences, interests, and available resources.

Additionally, the guide aims to provide practical information that can enhance the overall travel experience in Alaska. It offers insights into the local culture, customs, and etiquette, allowing visitors to better understand and appreciate the unique characteristics of the state. It also provides information on necessary permits or licenses for specific activities such as fishing or hunting, ensuring that travelers are aware of any legal requirements they need to fulfill.

Furthermore, the guide serves as a resource for travelers seeking information on outdoor activities and adventure opportunities in Alaska. It highlights popular hiking trails, wildlife viewing areas, national parks, and other natural wonders that make Alaska a sought-after destination for outdoor enthusiasts. By providing detailed descriptions of these attractions and activities, along with safety guidelines and recommendations, the guide helps travelers plan their itineraries effectively and make the most of their time in Alaska.

Overall, the purpose of the guide "Planning Your Trip to Alaska: Tips and Practical Information" is to empower travelers with comprehensive knowledge and practical advice that will enable them to plan a successful trip to Alaska. By addressing various aspects of travel planning and offering insights into local culture and outdoor activities, this book strives to provide tourists with an outstanding experience at one of the world's most gorgeous and awe-inspiring destinations.

CHAPTER 2

Understanding Alaska

Geography and Climate

As a traveler with knowledge, I can provide you with a comprehensive overview of the geography and climate of Alaska. Alaska is the largest state in the United States, located in the extreme northwest of North America. It is known for its vast wilderness, stunning landscapes, and unique climate.

Geography:

Alaska is bounded to the north by the Arctic Ocean, to the south and southwest by the Pacific Ocean, and to the east by Canada's Yukon Territory and British Columbia. The state covers an area of approximately 663,300 square miles (1,717,800 square kilometers), making it larger than Texas, California, and Montana combined. Due to its immense size, Alaska has a diverse range of geographical features.

The state can be divided into five major regions: the Southeast, Southcentral, Interior, Southwest, and Far North. The Southeast region is characterized by its fjords, islands, and temperate rainforests. It is home to the state capital Juneau and popular tourist destinations such as Glacier Bay National Park and Misty Fjords National Monument.

Southcentral Alaska is dominated by the Chugach Mountains and includes Anchorage, the largest city in the state. This region is known for its stunning coastal scenery, glaciers (including Portage Glacier), and abundant wildlife. The Kenai Peninsula is also located in Southcentral Alaska and offers opportunities for fishing, hiking, and wildlife viewing.

The Interior region of Alaska is characterized by vast stretches of tundra and boreal forests. It includes Denali National Park and Preserve, home to Mount McKinley (also known as Denali), the highest peak in North America. The Interior is sparsely populated but offers incredible opportunities for outdoor activities such as hiking, camping, and wildlife spotting.

The Southwest region of Alaska is known for its volcanic activity and rugged coastline. It includes the Aleutian Islands chain and Katmai National Park and Preserve, famous for its brown bears and the Valley of Ten Thousand Smokes, a volcanic landscape formed by the 1912 eruption of Novarupta.

The Far North region of Alaska is located above the Arctic Circle and experiences extreme cold temperatures. It is characterized by vast tundra plains, permafrost, and a unique ecosystem adapted to the harsh Arctic conditions. This region is home to the Arctic

National Wildlife Refuge and provides opportunities for Arctic exploration and wildlife observation.

Climate:

Alaska's climate varies greatly across its vast expanse. The state experiences a combination of subarctic and polar climates, with significant variations in temperature, precipitation, and daylight hours throughout the year.

In general, Alaska has long, cold winters and relatively short, cool summers. The coastal areas tend to have milder winters due to the moderating influence of the ocean, while the interior regions experience more extreme temperature fluctuations.

During winter, temperatures can drop well below freezing throughout the state. In some areas of the Interior and Far North, temperatures can reach as low as -50 degrees Fahrenheit (-45 degrees Celsius). The coastal regions have milder winter temperatures ranging from 20 to 30 degrees Fahrenheit (-7 to -1 degree Celsius).

Summer temperatures in Alaska vary depending on the region. Coastal areas typically have average highs in the 50s to 60s Fahrenheit (10 to 15 degrees Celsius), while interior regions can experience highs in the 70s to 80s Fahrenheit (20 to 30 degrees Celsius) during summer months.

Precipitation patterns also differ across Alaska. The coastal areas receive higher amounts of rainfall due to their proximity to the ocean, while interior regions are drier. The Southeast region is known for its abundant rainfall, with some areas receiving over 100 inches (254 centimeters) annually. In contrast, parts of the Interior and Far North receive less than 10 inches (25 centimeters) of precipitation per year.

Alaska is also known for its unique daylight patterns. During the summer months, especially in the Far North, the phenomenon known as the "Midnight Sun" occurs, where the sun remains above the horizon for 24 hours a day. Conversely, during winter, some areas experience extended periods of darkness with only a few hours of daylight.

Wildlife and Natural Wonders

Known for its vast wilderness and stunning landscapes, Alaska is home to a diverse range of wildlife and natural wonders that attract nature enthusiasts from around the world.

Wildlife in Alaska:

Alaska is renowned for its abundant wildlife, offering visitors the opportunity to observe various species in their natural habitats. One of the most iconic animals in Alaska is the grizzly bear (Ursus arctos horribilis). These majestic creatures can be found throughout the state, particularly in areas such as Denali National Park and Katmai National Park. Observing grizzly bears in their natural environment is an awe-inspiring experience that allows travelers to witness their impressive size and power.

Another notable species found in Alaska is the bald eagle (Haliaeetus leucocephalus). With its distinctive white head and impressive wingspan, the bald eagle is a symbol of American freedom and can be spotted along Alaska's coastlines and rivers. The Chilkat Bald Eagle Preserve near Haines is a popular destination for eagle watching, especially during the winter months when thousands of eagles gather to feed on salmon.

Alaska is also home to numerous marine mammals, including humpback whales (Megaptera novaeangliae), orcas (Orcinus orca), sea otters (Enhydra lutris), and harbor seals (Phoca vitulina). These magnificent creatures can be observed on boat tours or from coastal viewpoints. The Kenai Fjords National Park and Glacier Bay National Park are particularly renowned for their whale-watching opportunities.

Additionally, Alaska boasts an impressive array of bird species, making it a paradise for birdwatchers. The Arctic National Wildlife Refuge is a prime location for spotting migratory birds, including tundra swans, snow geese, and various species of waterfowl. The Pribilof Islands in the Bering Sea are famous for their seabird colonies, with millions of birds nesting on the cliffs, including puffins, kittiwakes, and cormorants.

Natural Wonders in Alaska:

Alaska is blessed with an abundance of natural wonders that showcase the state's raw beauty and untouched landscapes. One of the most famous natural wonders is Denali, formerly known as Mount McKinley, which is the highest peak in North America. Located within Denali National Park and Preserve, this majestic mountain offers breathtaking views and challenging hiking opportunities for adventurous travelers.

Glaciers are another prominent feature of Alaska's natural wonders. The state is home to numerous glaciers, including the famous Mendenhall Glacier near Juneau and the Hubbard Glacier in Yakutat Bay. These massive ice formations are a testament to the power of nature and provide visitors with a unique opportunity to witness the ever-changing landscape.

The Northern Lights, also known as the Aurora Borealis, are a mesmerizing natural phenomenon that can be seen in Alaska during the winter months. The dancing lights in the night sky create a magical spectacle that attracts photographers and nature enthusiasts from all over the world. Fairbanks and Anchorage are popular destinations for witnessing this awe-inspiring display of colors.

Alaska's national parks and wildlife refuges offer unparalleled opportunities to explore its natural wonders. Apart from Denali National Park, other notable parks include Kenai Fjords National Park, Glacier Bay National Park, and Wrangell-St. Elias National. These protected areas showcase Alaska's diverse ecosystems, including fjords, mountains, glaciers, and coastal regions.

In conclusion, Alaska is a haven for wildlife enthusiasts and nature lovers. Its diverse range of wildlife species, including grizzly bears, bald eagles, and marine mammals, offer unforgettable encounters in their natural habitats. The state's natural wonders, such as Denali, glaciers, and the Northern Lights, provide awe-inspiring experiences that showcase the raw beauty of Alaska's landscapes. Whether you are interested in observing wildlife or exploring breathtaking natural phenomena, Alaska offers an abundance of opportunities for an unforgettable journey.

Cultural Diversity

Cultural diversity in Alaska is a fascinating aspect that makes the state unique and rich in heritage. As a traveler with knowledge, I can provide you with comprehensive insights into the cultural diversity found in Alaska.

Alaska, known as "The Last Frontier," is home to a diverse range of cultures and ethnicities. The state's population consists of various indigenous groups, including the Inupiat, Yupik, Aleut,

Athabascan, Tlingit, Haida, and Tsimshian peoples. These indigenous communities have inhabited the region for thousands of years and have preserved their distinct cultural traditions and languages.

One of the prominent indigenous groups in Alaska is the Inupiat people. They primarily reside in the northern coastal areas of Alaska, such as Barrow (Utqiaġvik) and Kotzebue. The Inupiat have a deep connection to the land and sea, relying on subsistence hunting and fishing for their livelihoods. Their cultural practices revolve around whaling, seal hunting, gathering berries, and storytelling. Traditional dances like the blanket toss and drumming are integral parts of their cultural celebrations.

The Yupik people are another significant indigenous group in Alaska. They inhabit the southwestern coastal regions, including Bethel and Nome. The Yupik culture is closely tied to fishing, hunting marine mammals, and gathering wild plants. They have a rich artistic tradition that includes carving intricate masks, creating beautiful ivory carvings, and crafting traditional clothing adorned with intricate beadwork.

The Athabascan people are spread across interior Alaska, including Fairbanks and Fort Yukon. They have a deep spiritual connection to the land and rivers of Alaska. Their cultural practices involve subsistence hunting of moose, caribou, and small game animals.

The Athabascans are known for their skillful craftsmanship in creating birch bark baskets, beaded jewelry, and intricately designed traditional clothing.

The Tlingit, Haida, and Tsimshian peoples are indigenous groups primarily found in the southeastern region of Alaska, including Juneau and Ketchikan. These groups share cultural similarities and have a rich artistic heritage. They are renowned for their totem poles, intricate wood carvings, and vibrant ceremonial regalia. Potlatches, traditional feasts where gifts are exchanged, are an essential part of their cultural practices.

Apart from the indigenous communities, Alaska also has a diverse population of non-indigenous residents who have migrated from various parts of the United States and other countries. This diversity adds to the cultural tapestry of the state. Alaskans embrace their multicultural heritage through festivals, events, and community gatherings that celebrate different cultures.

The Alaska Native Heritage Center in Anchorage is a significant cultural institution that showcases the diverse indigenous cultures of Alaska. Visitors can learn about traditional practices, watch performances of native dances, and explore exhibits displaying artifacts and artwork. The center provides an immersive experience that highlights the importance of preserving and honoring Alaska's cultural diversity.

In conclusion, Alaska's cultural diversity is a testament to its rich history and heritage. The indigenous communities, with their distinct traditions and languages, form the foundation of this diversity. The Inupiat, Yupik, Aleut, Athabascan, Tlingit, Haida, and Tsimshian peoples have preserved their cultural practices for generations. Additionally, the state's non-indigenous population contributes to the multicultural fabric of Alaska. Exploring this cultural diversity as a traveler allows for a deeper understanding and appreciation of the unique experiences that Alaska has to offer.

CHAPTER 3

When to Go

Best Time to Visit Alaska

The timing of your visit can greatly impact the activities and attractions available to you, as well as the weather conditions you may encounter. Here is a detailed overview of the different seasons in Alaska and the factors to consider when planning your trip.

Summer (June to August):

Summer is the busiest season for tourists in Alaska, and for good reason. The weather is generally mild, with average temperatures ranging from 60°F to 80°F (15°C to 27°C) in most parts of the state. This is also the time when daylight hours are at their longest, providing ample time for outdoor activities and exploration.

One of the main highlights of visiting Alaska in summer is the opportunity to witness the midnight sun phenomenon. In northern parts of the state, such as Fairbanks and Barrow, the sun remains above the horizon for 24 hours a day during this period. This unique experience allows for extended daylight hours to enjoy activities like hiking, fishing, wildlife viewing, and taking scenic drives along Alaska's highways.

Summer is also an excellent time for wildlife enthusiasts, as many species are active during this season. You can spot bears fishing for salmon in rivers, observe whales in coastal areas, or witness migratory birds nesting and raising their young. Additionally, summer is when many festivals and events take place across Alaska, offering visitors a chance to immerse themselves in local culture.

Fall (September to October):

Fall in Alaska brings cooler temperatures and shorter daylight hours compared to summer. However, it is still a beautiful time to visit if you enjoy vibrant autumn foliage and fewer crowds. The landscapes transform into stunning shades of red, orange, and gold as the leaves change color.

During the fall, you can witness the spectacle of salmon spawning in rivers and streams, attracting bears and other wildlife. This is also a great time for fishing, as many fish species are preparing for winter and feeding voraciously. Additionally, fall is an ideal season for hiking and backpacking, as the trails are less crowded and the weather is generally mild.

Winter (November to March):

Winter in Alaska is a magical time, especially if you are interested in winter sports and unique natural phenomena. The state experiences long nights and shorter daylight hours during this season, with some areas experiencing polar nights where the sun does not rise above the horizon for several weeks.

Alaska is renowned for its winter activities such as dog sledding, snowmobiling, ice fishing, and skiing. The northern lights, also known as the aurora borealis, are another major attraction during winter. These mesmerizing light displays can be seen in clear night skies, particularly in more remote areas away from light pollution.

It's important to note that winter temperatures in Alaska can be extremely cold, ranging from -20°F to 20°F (-29°C to -6°C) or even lower in some regions. Proper clothing and equipment are essential to stay warm and safe while enjoying outdoor activities.

Spring (April to May):

Spring in Alaska is a transitional season characterized by melting snow and increasing daylight hours. Nature emerges from its winter slumber at this time of year. While temperatures can still be chilly, ranging from 30°F to 50°F (-1°C to 10°C), spring offers unique opportunities for wildlife viewing and birdwatching.

As the snow melts, rivers and waterfalls become more active, creating stunning photo opportunities. Spring is also the time when migratory birds return to Alaska after spending the winter in warmer climates. Birdwatchers can spot a wide variety of species as they arrive to nest and breed.

Overall, the best time to visit Alaska as a traveler depends on your personal preferences and the activities you wish to engage in. Summer offers longer daylight hours, milder temperatures, and a wide range of outdoor activities. Fall provides beautiful autumn foliage and fewer crowds. Winter offers unique winter sports and the chance to witness the northern lights. Spring brings the awakening of nature and opportunities for wildlife viewing.

When planning your trip, it's important to consider the specific regions of Alaska you wish to visit, as weather conditions can vary significantly across the state. Additionally, it's advisable to check with local authorities or tour operators for up-to-date information on road conditions, wildlife sightings, and any seasonal closures or restrictions.

Seasonal Considerations

As a traveler with experience, it is important to consider the seasonal variations when planning a trip to Alaska. The state's unique geography and climate offer a wide range of experiences throughout the year. Understanding the different seasons and their implications will help you make the most of your visit to this beautiful and diverse destination.

Summer (June to August):

In Alaska, the summer is the busiest travel period, and with good reason. The weather is generally mild, with temperatures ranging from 50°F to 70°F (10°C to 21°C) in most parts of the state. This is also the time when daylight hours are at their longest, providing ample time for outdoor activities and exploration.

One of the main attractions during summer is the opportunity to witness the midnight sun phenomenon, where the sun remains visible for almost 24 hours a day in some parts of Alaska. This unique experience allows for extended daylight hours, giving visitors more time to explore and enjoy outdoor activities such as hiking, fishing, wildlife viewing, and cruising.

However, it is important to note that summer is also the busiest time for tourism in Alaska. Popular destinations like Denali National Park and Kenai Fjords National Park can get crowded, and accommodations may be more expensive or harder to find without advance booking. Additionally, mosquitoes and other biting insects are prevalent during this season, so it is advisable to bring insect repellent.

Fall (September to November):

Fall in Alaska brings stunning displays of autumn foliage as the leaves change color. The temperatures start to drop, ranging from

30°F to 60°F (-1°C to 15°C), and daylight hours decrease significantly compared to summer. However, this season offers unique opportunities for wildlife viewing, as animals prepare for winter by migrating or gathering food.

September is particularly popular for visitors interested in witnessing the annual salmon run, where thousands of salmon swim upstream to spawn. This natural spectacle attracts not only tourists but also bears and other wildlife that feed on the abundant fish. Fall is also a great time for hiking, as the trails are less crowded compared to summer.

It is important to note that as fall progresses, the weather becomes more unpredictable, and some attractions and services may start closing for the winter season. It is advisable to check ahead for any closures or limited availability of activities and accommodations.

Winter (December to February):

Winter in Alaska is a magical time, with snow-covered landscapes and opportunities for unique experiences. The temperatures can range from -20°F to 30°F (-29°C to -1°C), depending on the region. The days are shorter, with some areas experiencing only a few hours of daylight or even complete darkness during the winter solstice.

One of the main attractions during winter is the opportunity to witness the mesmerizing Northern Lights (Aurora Borealis). Alaska's location within the auroral oval makes it one of the best places in the world to see this natural phenomenon. Fairbanks and other northern regions offer excellent viewing opportunities, especially on clear nights away from city lights.

Winter activities in Alaska include dog sledding, ice fishing, snowmobiling, skiing, and snowboarding. Many communities also celebrate winter festivals and events, showcasing local traditions and culture. However, it is important to be prepared for cold temperatures and potentially challenging weather conditions. Dressing in layers and having appropriate gear is essential for enjoying outdoor activities during this season.

Spring (March to May):

Spring in Alaska marks the transition from winter to summer, with temperatures gradually rising and daylight hours increasing. The weather can be unpredictable during this season, with temperatures ranging from 20°F to 50°F (-7°C to 10°C) in most areas.

As nature awakens from its winter slumber, spring provides a sense of rejuvenation. It is a great time for wildlife viewing, as animals emerge from hibernation and migratory birds return to their breeding grounds. The coastal areas become alive with marine life, including whales, sea lions, and seals.

However, it is important to note that some attractions and services may still be closed or have limited availability during the early spring months. It is advisable to check ahead for any seasonal closures or limited access to activities and accommodations.

In conclusion, Alaska offers a wide range of experiences throughout the year, each season bringing its own unique charm. Whether you visit during the summer to enjoy extended daylight hours and outdoor activities, witness the stunning fall foliage and wildlife migrations, experience the magical winter wonderland with the Northern Lights, or witness the awakening of nature in spring, Alaska has something to offer every traveler. Understanding the seasonal considerations will help you plan your trip accordingly and make the most of your visit to this breathtaking destination.

CHAPTER 4

Planning Your Itinerary

Duration of Stay

As a traveler with experience, planning your itinerary for visiting Alaska requires careful consideration of the duration of your stay. Alaska is a vast and diverse state, offering a wide range of attractions and activities that can cater to various interests. The duration of your stay will greatly impact the number of places you can visit and the experiences you can have.

The ideal duration of stay in Alaska depends on several factors, including your interests, budget, and the specific locations you wish to explore. However, a minimum of one week is recommended to truly immerse yourself in the beauty and adventure that Alaska has to offer

Alaska is known for its stunning natural landscapes, including glaciers, mountains, fjords, and national parks. If you are interested in exploring these natural wonders, it is advisable to allocate a significant portion of your itinerary to outdoor activities such as hiking, wildlife viewing, and scenic drives. The state's vast size means that travel times between destinations can be lengthy, so it is important to factor in transportation time when planning your itinerary.

One popular destination in Alaska is Denali National Park, home to North America's highest peak, Denali (formerly known as Mount McKinley). The park offers breathtaking views, diverse wildlife, and numerous hiking trails. To fully experience Denali National Park, it is recommended to spend at least two to three days exploring the park's various regions.

Another must-visit location in Alaska is the Kenai Peninsula. This region is renowned for its stunning coastal scenery, abundant wildlife, and world-class fishing opportunities. The Kenai Peninsula offers a range of activities such as kayaking, hiking, wildlife cruises, and visits to charming coastal towns like Seward and Homer. To fully appreciate the beauty of this area and engage in various activities, allocating three to four days would be ideal.

If you are interested in experiencing Alaska's marine life and glaciers up close, a visit to Southeast Alaska is highly recommended. This region is home to the Inside Passage, a scenic coastal route dotted with fjords, islands, and charming towns like Juneau, Skagway, and Ketchikan. To explore the highlights of Southeast Alaska, including Glacier Bay National Park and Tracy Arm Fjord, it is advisable to spend at least four to five days in the region.

In addition to these specific destinations, Alaska offers numerous other attractions and activities that may pique your interest. These include exploring the Arctic region, visiting remote villages, experiencing dog sledding, and witnessing the Northern Lights. The duration of your stay should be adjusted accordingly if you wish to include these unique experiences in your itinerary.

It is important to note that Alaska's weather can be unpredictable, with long daylight hours during the summer months and colder temperatures during the winter. When planning your itinerary, consider the season in which you will be visiting and pack appropriate clothing and gear.

In conclusion, the duration of your stay in Alaska should be based on your interests, budget, and the specific locations you wish to explore. While a minimum of one week is recommended to fully appreciate the beauty and adventure that Alaska has to offer, allocating more time will allow for a more comprehensive exploration of this vast state.

Choosing Destinations

When planning a trip to Alaska, it is essential to carefully choose your destinations and create an itinerary that allows you to make the most of your time in this vast and diverse state. As a traveler with experience, I can provide you with some valuable insights on how to choose the best destinations for your Alaska adventure.

Consider Your Interests and Preferences:

The first step in planning your itinerary is to consider your interests and preferences. Alaska offers a wide range of activities and attractions, so it's important to identify what you want to experience during your trip. Are you interested in wildlife viewing, hiking, fishing, or cultural experiences? Do you prefer remote wilderness areas or bustling cities? Understanding your preferences will help you narrow down the destinations that align with your interests.

Research the Different Regions:

Alaska is divided into several distinct regions, each offering unique landscapes and attractions. Some of the very popular regions are:

- Southeast Alaska: Known as the Inside Passage, this region is famous for its stunning fjords, glaciers, and abundant wildlife. It is home to popular destinations such as Juneau, Ketchikan, and Skagway. Cruising through the Inside Passage is a popular way to explore this region.
- Southcentral Alaska: This region is home to Anchorage, the largest city in Alaska, as well as the stunning Kenai Peninsula. Southcentral Alaska offers a mix of urban amenities and outdoor adventures, including hiking in Chugach State Park, fishing in the Kenai River, or visiting the charming town of Seward.

- Interior Alaska: The interior region is known for its vast wilderness areas and iconic national parks such as Denali National Park and Preserve. If you're interested in wildlife viewing or hiking in pristine landscapes, this region should be on your list.
- Arctic Alaska: For those seeking a truly remote and untouched experience, Arctic Alaska is the place to go. This region offers unique opportunities to witness the Northern Lights, explore the Arctic tundra, and learn about the indigenous cultures that call this area home.

Prioritize Must-See Attractions:

Once you have an idea of the regions you want to visit, it's time to prioritize the must-see attractions within each region. Alaska is known for its breathtaking natural beauty, so make sure to include some of the following attractions in your itinerary:

- Denali National Park and Preserve: Home to North America's highest peak, Denali (formerly known as Mount McKinley), this national park offers unparalleled opportunities for wildlife viewing, hiking, and mountaineering.
- Glacier Bay National Park and Preserve: A UNESCO World Heritage Site, Glacier Bay is a stunning wilderness

area where you can witness massive glaciers calving into the sea and spot marine wildlife such as whales and seals.

- Kenai Fjords National Park: Located on the Kenai Peninsula, this national park is famous for its rugged coastline, fjords, and abundant marine life. Take a boat tour to explore the park's glaciers and spot wildlife like sea otters and puffins.
- Mendenhall Glacier: Located near Juneau in Southeast Alaska, Mendenhall Glacier is easily accessible and offers a chance to witness the power of glacial ice up close. Take a hike or kayak tour to fully experience this natural wonder.

Consider Practicalities:

When planning your itinerary, it's important to consider practicalities such as transportation options, accommodation availability, and seasonal variations. Alaska's vast size and remote locations can make logistics challenging, so plan ahead and book accommodations and transportation well in advance. Additionally, be aware of the weather conditions during your visit as they can greatly impact your travel plans.

In conclusion, choosing destinations in planning your itinerary for visiting Alaska requires careful consideration of your interests, researching the different regions, prioritizing must-see attractions, and considering practicalities such as transportation and accommodation. By following these steps, you can create an itinerary that allows you to make the most of your Alaska adventure.

Transportation Options

Transportation options in Alaska are diverse and unique due to the state's vast size, rugged terrain, and remote locations. The transportation infrastructure in Alaska is designed to cater to the needs of both residents and tourists, ensuring connectivity across the state. This comprehensive guide will explore the various modes of transportation available in Alaska, including air travel, roadways, railways, ferries, and alternative options.

Air Travel:

Air travel is a crucial mode of transportation in Alaska due to its expansive geography and limited road access. The state has numerous airports, ranging from major international airports to smaller regional and local airstrips. Ted Stevens Anchorage International Airport is the largest airport in Alaska and serves as a major hub for both domestic and international flights. Other significant airports include Fairbanks International Airport, Juneau International Airport, and Ketchikan International Airport.

Alaska Airlines is the primary carrier serving the state, offering flights to various destinations within Alaska as well as connections to other parts of the United States. Additionally, several smaller regional airlines operate in Alaska, providing essential air services to remote communities that are inaccessible by road.

Roadways:

Alaska has an extensive road network that connects major cities and towns. The most famous highway in the state is the Alaska Highway (also known as the Alcan Highway), which stretches over 1,400 miles from Dawson Creek, British Columbia, to Delta Junction, Alaska. This highway provides a vital land link between Alaska and the contiguous United States.

The George Parks Highway connects Anchorage with Denali National Park and Fairbanks. The Seward Highway connects Anchorage with Seward on the Kenai Peninsula, offering breathtaking views of mountains and coastal scenery along the way. Other notable highways include the Richardson Highway, Glenn Highway, and Dalton Highway.

It's important to note that road conditions can vary significantly throughout Alaska due to weather conditions and maintenance schedules. Travelers should be prepared for potential hazards such as wildlife crossings, icy roads, and limited services in remote areas.

Railways:

The Alaska Railroad is a scenic railway system that spans approximately 500 miles from Seward to Fairbanks. This iconic rail line offers passengers a unique way to experience Alaska's stunning landscapes, including mountains, glaciers, and wildlife. The Alaska Railroad operates both passenger and freight services, with stops at various towns and attractions along the route.

Passenger trains provide comfortable seating, large windows for optimal viewing, and onboard amenities. The Denali Star is the flagship train that runs between Anchorage and Fairbanks, passing through Denali National Park. Other routes include the Coastal Classic (Anchorage to Seward) and the Glacier Discovery (Anchorage to Whittier or Spencer Glacier).

Ferries:

Alaska's marine highway system is an essential transportation option for coastal communities and visitors looking to explore the state's stunning coastline. The Alaska Marine Highway System (AMHS) operates a fleet of ferries that connect over 30 communities along the Inside Passage, Southcentral, and Southwest regions of Alaska.

The ferries offer both passenger and vehicle transportation, allowing travelers to bring their cars or RVs on board. This mode of transportation provides a scenic journey through fjords, islands, and coastal mountains while offering opportunities for wildlife viewing. Major ports served by the AMHS include Ketchikan, Juneau, Sitka, Haines, Skagway, Valdez, Kodiak, and Dutch Harbor.

Alternative Options:

In addition to traditional modes of transportation, Alaska offers some unique alternatives for getting around the state:

- Dog Sledding: Dog sledding is an iconic Alaskan activity that allows travelers to experience the thrill of mushing through snow-covered landscapes. Several tour operators offer dog sledding experiences in popular tourist destinations like Anchorage, Fairbanks, and Denali National Park.
- Snowmobiles: Snowmobiles, also known as snow machines in Alaska, are a popular means of transportation and recreation during the winter months. They provide access to remote areas and allow for thrilling adventures across the state's snowy terrain.
- Bush Planes: In remote areas with limited or no road access, bush planes are often used for transportation. These small aircraft can land on short runways or even

unimproved landing strips, providing essential services to remote communities, lodges, and wilderness areas.

In conclusion, Alaska offers a wide range of transportation options to accommodate the unique needs of its residents and visitors. Air travel is essential for connecting major cities and remote communities, while roadways provide access to various destinations within the state. The Alaska Railroad offers a scenic journey through breathtaking landscapes, and the marine highway system allows for coastal exploration. Additionally, alternative options like dog sledding, snowmobiles, and bush planes provide unique experiences in this vast and rugged state.

CHAPTER 5

Accommodation Options

Hotels and Resorts

Hotels and Resorts in Alaska offer visitors a wide range of options to choose from, catering to different budgets and preferences. Whether you are looking for a luxurious resort or a cozy hotel, Alaska has something to offer for everyone. In this comprehensive guide, we will explore some of the top hotels and resorts in Alaska, along with their costs and locations.

Alyeska Resort:

Located in Girdwood, Alyeska Resort is a premier destination for both winter and summer activities. The resort offers luxurious accommodations with stunning views of the surrounding mountains and glaciers. The Hotel Alyeska features 304 rooms and suites, each elegantly furnished with modern amenities. The resort also boasts a variety of dining options, including fine dining at Seven Glaciers restaurant, casual fare at the Pond Café, and après-ski drinks at the Sitzmark Bar & Grill. Other amenities include a spa, fitness center, indoor pool, and hot tub. The cost of staying at Alyeska Resort varies depending on the season and room type, with prices ranging from $200 to $600 per night.

Captain Cook Hotel:

Situated in downtown Anchorage, the Captain Cook Hotel is a landmark property known for its exceptional service and convenient location. The hotel offers 546 guest rooms and suites, each featuring modern amenities and comfortable furnishings. Guests can enjoy panoramic views of the city or the Chugach Mountains from their rooms. The hotel is home to several restaurants, including the Crow's Nest on the top floor, which offers breathtaking views of the surrounding area while serving gourmet cuisine. Other amenities include a fitness center, spa services, and an indoor pool. The cost of staying at the Captain Cook Hotel ranges from $150 to $400 per night.

Talkeetna Alaskan Lodge:

Nestled in the small town of Talkeetna, the Talkeetna Alaskan Lodge offers a rustic yet luxurious experience in the heart of nature. The lodge features 212 guest rooms and cabins, each designed to provide a cozy and comfortable stay. Guests can enjoy stunning views of Denali (Mount McKinley) and the Alaska Range from their rooms or the lodge's expansive deck. The Foraker Dining Room serves delicious Alaskan cuisine made with locally sourced ingredients, while the Base Camp Bistro offers casual dining options. Other amenities include a gift shop, outdoor hot tubs, and access to hiking trails. The cost of staying at the Talkeetna Alaskan Lodge ranges from $200 to $500 per night.

Hotel Captain Cook:

Another notable hotel in Anchorage is the Hotel Captain Cook, located in downtown Anchorage. This iconic hotel offers a range of accommodations, including deluxe rooms, suites, and executive apartments. Each room is tastefully designed and equipped with modern conveniences. The hotel features several restaurants, including the Crow's Nest on the top floor, which offers panoramic views of the city and surrounding mountains. Other amenities include a fitness center, spa services, and an indoor pool. The cost of staying at the Hotel Captain Cook varies depending on the room type and season, with prices ranging from $150 to $400 per night.

Glacier Bay Lodge:

For those looking to explore Glacier Bay National Park, Glacier Bay Lodge is an excellent choice. Located in Gustavus, this lodge offers comfortable accommodations with breathtaking views of the surrounding wilderness. The lodge features 56 guest rooms, each with private bathrooms and modern amenities. Guests can enjoy meals at the Westmark Bar & Grill or grab a quick bite at the Glacier Bay Lodge Café. The lodge also offers various activities and excursions to explore the park's glaciers and wildlife. The cost of staying at Glacier Bay Lodge ranges from $200 to $400 per night.

These are just a few examples of the many hotels and resorts available in Alaska. The cost of staying at each establishment can vary depending on factors such as the season, room type, and availability. It is always recommended to check with the specific hotel or resort for the most up-to-date pricing information.

Lodges and Cabins

Alaska, known for its stunning natural beauty and abundant wildlife, offers a wide range of lodges and cabins for visitors to enjoy a unique and immersive experience in the Last Frontier. Whether you are seeking a remote wilderness retreat or a cozy cabin near a bustling town, Alaska has something to offer for every type of traveler. In this comprehensive guide, we will explore some of the top lodges and cabins in Alaska, including their locations and costs.

Tutka Bay Lodge:

Located on the rugged coastline of the Kenai Peninsula, Tutka Bay Lodge is a luxurious wilderness retreat that offers breathtaking views of Kachemak Bay. Accessible only by boat or seaplane, this lodge provides an exclusive and secluded experience for its guests. The lodge features comfortable cabins with modern amenities, gourmet dining options, and a variety of outdoor activities such as kayaking, hiking, and wildlife viewing. The cost of staying at Tutka Bay Lodge starts at around $1,500 per night.

Denali Backcountry Lodge:

Nestled deep within Denali National Park, Denali Backcountry Lodge offers an unparalleled opportunity to explore the pristine wilderness surrounding North America's tallest peak. The lodge is accessible via a scenic bus ride from the park entrance and provides rustic yet comfortable accommodations in cozy cabins. Guests can enjoy guided hikes, wildlife tours, and educational programs led by knowledgeable naturalists. The cost of staying at Denali Backcountry Lodge starts at around $400 per night.

Chena Hot Springs Resort:

Situated about 60 miles northeast of Fairbanks, Chena Hot Springs Resort is renowned for its natural hot springs and aurora viewing opportunities. The resort offers a range of accommodations including cabins, yurts, and rooms in the main lodge. Guests can soak in the healing waters of the hot springs, take part in guided tours, and even witness the mesmerizing Northern Lights during the winter months. The cost of staying at Chena Hot Springs Resort varies depending on the type of accommodation chosen, with prices starting at around $150 per night.

Kenai Fjords Wilderness Lodge:

Located on Fox Island in Resurrection Bay, Kenai Fjords Wilderness Lodge provides a remote and serene escape surrounded by glaciers, fjords, and abundant marine wildlife. Accessible only by boat from Seward, this lodge offers comfortable cabins with stunning ocean views. Guests can enjoy guided kayak tours, wildlife cruises, and hiking excursions in the nearby Kenai Fjords National Park. The cost of staying at Kenai Fjords Wilderness Lodge starts at around $500 per night.

Kantishna Roadhouse:

Situated deep within Denali National Park, Kantishna Roadhouse offers a true wilderness experience with its remote location and rustic accommodations. Guests can reach the lodge via a scenic bus ride through the park's rugged terrain. The lodge features cozy cabins with private bathrooms and a range of activities including guided hikes, gold panning, and wildlife viewing. The cost of staying at Kantishna Roadhouse starts at around $400 per night.

Alaska's Gold Creek Lodge:

Located in the heart of the Bristol Bay region, Alaska's Gold Creek Lodge offers a unique combination of wilderness adventure and world-class fishing opportunities. The lodge provides comfortable cabins overlooking the Kvichak River and Lake Iliamna. Guests can enjoy fly fishing for salmon and trout, as well as participate in bear viewing tours and scenic flights over the surrounding area. The cost of staying at Alaska's Gold Creek Lodge starts at around $600 per night.

Winterlake Lodge:

Nestled along the Iditarod Trail in the Alaska Range, Winterlake Lodge offers a remote and luxurious retreat for those seeking tranquility and adventure. Accessible by floatplane from Anchorage, this lodge provides cozy cabins with stunning views of the surrounding mountains and lakes. Guests can indulge in gourmet cuisine, go dog sledding, take helicopter tours to nearby glaciers, and relax in the lodge's wood-fired sauna. The cost of staying at Winterlake Lodge starts at around $1,200 per night.

These are just a few examples of the many lodges and cabins available in Alaska. It is important to note that prices mentioned above are approximate and can vary depending on the season, availability, and specific package options offered by each establishment. Additionally, it is recommended to make reservations well in advance, especially during peak travel seasons.

Camping and RV Parks

Camping and RV parks in Alaska offer a unique opportunity to experience the stunning natural beauty of the Last Frontier. With its vast wilderness, towering mountains, pristine lakes, and abundant wildlife, Alaska is a dream destination for outdoor enthusiasts. Whether you prefer tent camping or traveling in an RV, there are numerous parks and campgrounds throughout the state that cater to different preferences and budgets.

Denali National Park and Preserve:

Located in the interior of Alaska, Denali National Park and Preserve is a popular destination for camping and RV enthusiasts. The park offers six campgrounds, each with its own unique features and amenities. The Riley Creek Campground is the largest campground in the park and offers both tent and RV sites. It is open year-round and provides access to hiking trails, visitor centers, and shuttle buses. The cost for camping at Riley Creek Campground is $28 per night for a tent site and $34 per night for an RV site with electric hookups.

Chugach State Park:

Situated near Anchorage, Chugach State Park is the third-largest state park in the United States. It offers a wide range of recreational activities, including camping, hiking, fishing, and wildlife viewing. There are several campgrounds within the park that accommodate both tents and RVs. Eagle River Campground is one of the most popular options, offering beautiful views of the surrounding mountains and easy access to hiking trails. The cost for camping at Eagle River Campground is $20 per night for a tent site and $30 per night for an RV site with electric hookups.

Kenai Fjords National Park:

Located on the Kenai Peninsula in southern Alaska, Kenai Fjords National Park is known for its stunning glaciers, fjords, and abundant marine wildlife. The park offers two campgrounds: Exit Glacier Campground and Resurrection River Campground. Exit Glacier Campground is the more developed option, offering tent and RV sites with access to restrooms, water, and picnic tables. The cost for camping at Exit Glacier Campground is $14 per night for a tent site and $22 per night for an RV site with electric hookups.

Tongass National Forest:

As the largest national forest in the United States, Tongass National Forest covers a vast area of southeastern Alaska. It offers numerous camping opportunities, including both developed campgrounds and remote backcountry sites. Some popular campgrounds within Tongass National Forest include Mendenhall Lake Campground near Juneau, Ward Lake Recreation Area near Ketchikan, and Anan Bay Cabin near Wrangell. The cost for camping in Tongass National Forest varies depending on the specific campground and amenities provided.

Wrangell-St. Elias National Park and Preserve:

Wrangell-St. Elias National Park and Preserve is the United States' largest national park, comprising over 13 million acres of harsh wilderness. The park offers several campgrounds that cater to different types of camping experiences. For RV camping, the park recommends staying at the Nabesna Road Campground or the Slana Ranger Station Campground. Both campgrounds offer basic amenities such as pit toilets and picnic tables. The cost for camping at these campgrounds is $10 per night.

CHAPTER 6

Getting There

Air Travel to Alaska

Air travel to Alaska for visitors is a popular mode of transportation due to the state's remote location and vast wilderness. Alaska, known for its stunning landscapes, wildlife, and outdoor activities, attracts tourists from around the world. Whether you are planning a vacation or a business trip to Alaska, understanding the various aspects of air travel to the state can help ensure a smooth and enjoyable experience.

Booking Flights to Alaska:

When planning air travel to Alaska, the first step is to book your flights. There are several major airlines that offer regular service to Alaska, including Alaska Airlines, Delta Air Lines, United Airlines, and American Airlines. These airlines provide both domestic and international flights to various cities in Alaska, such as Anchorage, Fairbanks, Juneau, and Sitka.

To find the best deals on flights to Alaska, it is recommended to use online travel agencies or airline websites that allow you to compare prices and schedules. Additionally, signing up for airline newsletters or following them on social media platforms can provide you with information about special promotions or discounts.

Choosing Airports in Alaska:

Alaska has several airports that serve as entry points for visitors. The largest and busiest airport in the state is Ted Stevens Anchorage International Airport (ANC), located in Anchorage. This airport offers numerous domestic and international flights and serves as a hub for connecting flights within the state.

Other major airports in Alaska include Fairbanks International Airport (FAI) in Fairbanks and Juneau International Airport (JNU) in Juneau. These airports also have regular flights from various destinations and provide convenient access to different regions of the state.

Flight Duration and Connections:

The duration of flights to Alaska depends on your departure location. For example, if you are flying from Seattle, Washington, the flight duration to Anchorage is approximately 3 hours. However, if you are traveling from a more distant location like New York City or Los Angeles, the flight duration can range from 5 to 7 hours.

It is important to note that direct flights to Alaska may not be available from all locations. In such cases, connecting flights are necessary. Common connection cities for flights to Alaska include Seattle, Portland, Denver, and Minneapolis. When booking your flights, make sure to consider layover times and plan accordingly.

Travel Documents and Customs:

When traveling to Alaska from another country, it is essential to have the necessary travel documents. Visitors from outside the United States must possess a valid passport and may require a visa depending on their nationality. It is recommended to check the U.S. Department of State's website or consult with your local embassy or consulate for specific entry requirements.

Upon arrival in Alaska, all visitors must go through customs and immigration procedures. Be prepared to present your passport, completed customs declaration form, and any required visas or permits. It is advisable to familiarize yourself with the customs regulations of both your home country and the United States to avoid any issues during the entry process.

Baggage Allowance and Restrictions:

Each airline has its own baggage allowance policy, so it is important to check with your chosen airline regarding their specific rules and restrictions. Generally, airlines allow passengers to bring one carry-on bag and one personal item (such as a purse or laptop bag) free of charge. Checked baggage allowances vary depending on the airline, ticket class, and destination.

It is crucial to adhere to the airline's restrictions on baggage size, weight limits, and prohibited items. Some common restricted items include sharp objects, flammable materials, firearms, and certain types of liquids. Familiarize yourself with these regulations before packing to avoid any inconvenience or delays at the airport.

Weather Considerations:

Alaska's weather can be unpredictable and varies significantly depending on the region and time of year. It is advisable to check the weather forecast for your destination in Alaska before traveling. This will help you pack appropriate clothing and gear for the conditions you may encounter.

During the winter months, temperatures in Alaska can drop well below freezing, especially in the interior and northern regions. It is essential to dress in layers and have warm clothing, including a good quality winter coat, hats, gloves, and insulated footwear. In the summer, temperatures can range from mild to warm, but it is still recommended to bring a light jacket or sweater for cooler evenings.

Transportation within Alaska:

Once you arrive in Alaska, there are various transportation options available to explore the state. Rental cars are a popular choice for visitors who want the flexibility to travel at their own pace. However, it is important to note that some areas of Alaska may have limited road access or require specialized vehicles like four-wheel drives.

Alternatively, public transportation options such as buses and trains are available in certain regions. For example, the Alaska Railroad offers scenic train rides that connect major cities and towns throughout the state. Additionally, there are tour operators that provide guided tours and transportation services to popular tourist destinations.

Cruising to Alaska

Cruising to Alaska is a popular choice for visitors looking to explore the stunning natural beauty and unique wildlife of this remote region. With its towering glaciers, majestic fjords, and abundant wildlife, Alaska offers a truly unforgettable cruising experience. In this comprehensive guide, we will delve into the various aspects of cruising to Alaska, including the best time to visit, popular cruise routes, must-see attractions, and practical tips for planning your trip.

Best Time to Visit:

Alaska's cruising season typically runs from May to September, with the peak months being June, July, and August. During this time, the weather is relatively mild, and the days are long, allowing for more time to explore ashore. However, it's important to note that Alaska's weather can be unpredictable, so it's always a good idea to pack layers and be prepared for changing conditions.

Popular Cruise Routes:

There are several popular cruise routes in Alaska that offer different experiences and itineraries. The most common route is the Inside Passage, which takes you through a network of islands and fjords along the southeastern coast of Alaska. This route often includes stops at ports such as Juneau, Ketchikan, Skagway, and Glacier Bay National Park.

Another popular option is the Gulf of Alaska route, which typically starts or ends in Vancouver or Seattle and takes you through the scenic waters of the Gulf of Alaska. This route often includes stops at ports such as Anchorage (Whittier), Hubbard Glacier, and College Fjord.

For those looking for a more adventurous experience, there are also expedition cruises that venture into more remote areas of Alaska such as the Aleutian Islands or the Bering Sea. These cruises offer opportunities for wildlife viewing and exploring lesser-known destinations.

Must-See Attractions:

Alaska is known for its breathtaking natural beauty and unique wildlife. Some of the must-see attractions during a cruise to Alaska include:

Glacier Bay National Park: This UNESCO World Heritage Site is home to some of the most spectacular glaciers in Alaska. Cruising through Glacier Bay allows you to witness the immense beauty of these icy giants and spot wildlife such as humpback whales, sea lions, and bald eagles.

Denali National Park: Located in the interior of Alaska, Denali National Park is home to North America's tallest peak, Mount McKinley (also known as Denali). A visit to this park offers opportunities for wildlife viewing, hiking, and taking in the stunning mountain scenery.

Tracy Arm Fjord: This narrow fjord located near Juneau is renowned for its towering cliffs, cascading waterfalls, and floating icebergs. Cruising through Tracy Arm allows you to get up close to the Sawyer Glaciers and witness the raw beauty of this untouched wilderness.

Practical Tips for Planning Your Trip:

Here are some practical tips to help you plan your cruise to Alaska:

- Research and book your cruise early: Alaska cruises tend to fill up quickly, especially during the peak season. It's advisable to book your cruise well in advance to secure your preferred dates and cabin category.
- Pack appropriate clothing: Alaska's weather can be unpredictable, so it's important to pack layers and bring waterproof outerwear. Be prepared for both warm and cold temperatures, as well as rain.
- Consider shore excursions: Many cruise lines offer a variety of shore excursions that allow you to explore Alaska's natural wonders up close. From whale watching tours to helicopter rides over glaciers, there are plenty of options to enhance your experience.
- Take advantage of onboard activities: Most cruise ships sailing to Alaska offer a range of onboard activities and entertainment options. From educational lectures about the region's wildlife and history to live performances showcasing local culture, there's something for everyone to enjoy.

In conclusion, cruising to Alaska offers visitors a unique opportunity to explore one of the world's most breathtaking destinations. From the stunning glaciers and fjords to the abundant wildlife and rich cultural heritage, Alaska has something to offer every traveler. By planning your trip well in advance, packing appropriately, and taking advantage of shore excursions and onboard activities, you can make the most of your Alaskan cruise experience.

Driving to Alaska

Driving to Alaska can be an exciting and adventurous journey for visitors. The vast landscapes, stunning natural beauty, and unique experiences along the way make it a memorable road trip. However, it is important to plan and prepare adequately for such a long-distance drive. In this comprehensive guide, we will provide you with all the necessary information and tips to make your drive to Alaska a safe and enjoyable experience.

Planning the Route:

Before embarking on your journey, it is crucial to plan your route carefully. There are several options available depending on your starting point and preferences. The most common routes include driving through Canada or taking a ferry from Washington State to Alaska.

- Driving through Canada: If you are coming from the contiguous United States, driving through Canada is the most popular option. The primary route is known as the Alaska Highway or the Alcan Highway. It runs from Dawson Creek, British Columbia, to Delta Junction, Alaska. This route covers approximately 1,387 miles (2,232 kilometers) and offers breathtaking views of mountains, forests, and wildlife along the way.
- Taking a ferry: Another option is to take a ferry from Washington State to Alaska. The Alaska Marine Highway System operates ferries that connect various coastal communities in Alaska with Bellingham, Washington. This option allows you to bring your vehicle onboard and enjoy a scenic journey through the Inside Passage.

Preparing Your Vehicle:

Driving to Alaska requires proper preparation of your vehicle to ensure its reliability throughout the trip. Here are some important procedures to take before you hit the road:

- Vehicle maintenance: Schedule a thorough inspection of your vehicle before the trip. Check the tires, brakes, fluids, lights, and other crucial components to ensure they are in good condition. Consider getting an oil change and replacing any worn-out parts.

- Emergency kit: Pack an emergency kit that includes essential items such as a spare tire, jack, jumper cables, flashlight, first aid supplies, and extra food and water. It is also advisable to carry a basic toolkit and a fire extinguisher.
- Documentation: Make sure to carry all necessary documents, including your driver's license, vehicle registration, proof of insurance, and passport (if driving through Canada). Additionally, inform your insurance company about your travel plans to ensure coverage in case of any unforeseen incidents.

Road Conditions and Safety:

Driving to Alaska involves traversing long distances through remote areas with varying road conditions. It is crucial to prioritize safety and be prepared for potential challenges. Here are some important considerations:

- Weather conditions: Alaska's weather can be unpredictable, especially in the northern regions. Be prepared for rain, snow, fog, and strong winds. Check weather forecasts on a frequent basis and make necessary adjustments to your plans. Carry appropriate clothing and equipment for different weather conditions.

- Road maintenance: The Alaska Highway is generally well-maintained; however, it is essential to be aware of potential road hazards such as potholes, construction zones, and wildlife crossings. Slow down when encountering these situations and follow any posted signs or instructions.
- Fuel and services: Gas stations and services may be limited in certain areas along the route. Plan your fuel stops accordingly and carry extra fuel if necessary. It is also advisable to stock up on food, water, and other supplies in case of unexpected delays or closures.

Attractions and Points of Interest:

Driving to Alaska offers numerous opportunities to explore breathtaking landscapes and unique attractions along the way. Here are some notable points of interest that you may consider visiting:

- Yukon Territory: As you drive through Canada, make sure to explore the stunning wilderness of the Yukon Territory. Visit Kluane National Park and Reserve, home to Canada's highest peak Mount Logan. Take a detour to Whitehorse, the capital city of Yukon, and experience its rich history and vibrant arts scene.
- Denali National Park: Located in Alaska, Denali National Park is a must-visit destination. Marvel at the majestic Mount McKinley (also known as Denali), North America's

highest peak. Enjoy wildlife viewing, hiking trails, and breathtaking scenery in this pristine wilderness.

- Kenai Peninsula: Drive south from Anchorage to the Kenai Peninsula, known for its stunning coastline and abundant wildlife. Explore the charming town of Seward, go fishing in the Kenai River, or take a boat tour to witness glaciers calving into the ocean in Kenai Fjords National Park.

In conclusion, driving to Alaska can be an incredible adventure for visitors. By planning your route, preparing your vehicle, prioritizing safety, and exploring the attractions along the way, you can make this road trip a truly memorable experience.

CHAPTER 7

Visa and Entry Requirements

Passport Requirements

Alaska, the largest state in the United States, is a popular destination for tourists from around the world. If you are planning a trip to Alaska, it is important to understand the passport requirements for visitors. This comprehensive guide will provide you with all the necessary information regarding passport requirements to Alaska.

Passport Basics:

A passport is a government-issued document that certifies a person's identification and citizenship. It serves as a travel document that allows individuals to enter and exit foreign countries. When traveling to Alaska, visitors must ensure they have a valid passport that meets the requirements set by the U.S. government.

Passport Validity:

To enter Alaska as a visitor, your passport must be valid for at least six months beyond your intended stay. This requirement ensures that visitors have a valid travel document throughout their entire trip and allows for any unforeseen circumstances or delays that may occur during their stay.

Visa Waiver Program:

The Visa Waiver Program (VWP) enables nationals of certain nations to visit the United States for vacation or business without obtaining a visa.

However, even if you are eligible for the VWP, you still need to have a valid Electronic System for Travel Authorization (ESTA) approval before traveling to Alaska or any other part of the United States.

Visa Requirements:

If you are not eligible for the Visa Waiver Program or if you plan to stay in Alaska for longer than 90 days, you will need to apply for a visa. The type of visa required will depend on the purpose of your visit, such as tourism, business, or study. It is essential to check with the nearest U.S. embassy or consulate in your country of residence to determine the specific visa requirements and application process.

Passport Exemptions:

There are certain exemptions to passport requirements when traveling to Alaska. These exemptions apply to U.S. citizens, U.S.

nationals, and individuals who are eligible for entry under the Western Hemisphere Travel Initiative (WHTI). The WHTI allows citizens of the United States, Canada, Mexico, Bermuda, and the Caribbean countries to travel within these regions using alternative documents such as an enhanced driver's license or a trusted traveler program card.

Passport Renewal:

If your passport is nearing its expiration date or has already expired, it is crucial to renew it before traveling to Alaska. You can renew your passport by contacting the American embassy or consulate in your country of residency. It is recommended to start the renewal process well in advance to avoid any last-minute complications.

Traveling with Children:

When traveling with children to Alaska, it is important to note that they must have their own valid passports. Previously, children could be included on a parent's passport; however, this policy has changed, and each child now requires their own individual passport.

Additional Considerations:

While having a valid passport is the primary requirement for visiting Alaska, there are a few additional considerations to keep in mind:

- Identification Requirements: In addition to a passport, visitors may be required to present additional identification documents upon arrival in Alaska. This can include a driver's license or national identity card.
- Customs and Border Protection: Visitors should familiarize themselves with the customs and border protection regulations of both their home country and the United States. This will help ensure a smooth entry into Alaska and compliance with all necessary procedures.

In conclusion, when planning a trip to Alaska as a visitor, it is crucial to have a valid passport that meets the requirements set by the U.S. government. Additionally, it is important to be aware of any visa requirements, exemptions, and other considerations that may apply to your specific situation. By ensuring you have the necessary travel documents in order, you can enjoy a hassle-free visit to the beautiful state of Alaska.

Visa Regulations

Visa regulations for visitors to Alaska depend on the nationality of the visitor and the purpose of their visit. The United States has a visa waiver program that allows citizens of certain countries to travel to the U.S., including Alaska, for tourism or business purposes without obtaining a visa. However, citizens of other countries may need to apply for a visa before traveling to Alaska.

For citizens of countries participating in the Visa Waiver Program (VWP), they are eligible to travel to Alaska without a visa if they meet certain requirements. These requirements include having a valid Electronic System for Travel Authorization (ESTA) approval, which can be obtained online prior to travel. The ESTA is valid for multiple entries within a two-year period or until the passport expires, whichever comes first. Visitors must also have a machine-readable passport and their stay in Alaska must not exceed 90 days.

Citizens of countries not participating in the Visa Waiver Program are required to obtain a nonimmigrant visa before traveling to Alaska. The kind of visa needed will depend on the visit's purpose. The most common types of nonimmigrant visas for visitors to Alaska include:

- B-1 Business Visitor Visa: This visa is for individuals traveling to Alaska for business purposes such as attending conferences, meetings, or negotiating contracts.
- B-2 Tourist Visa: This visa is for individuals traveling to Alaska for tourism or recreational purposes such as sightseeing, visiting friends or relatives, or participating in social events.

To apply for a nonimmigrant visa, visitors must complete the online application form (DS-160) and schedule an interview at the nearest U.S. embassy or consulate in their home country. During the interview, applicants will be required to provide supporting documents such as a valid passport, proof of financial ability to support themselves during their stay in Alaska, and evidence of ties to their home country that would compel them to return after their visit.

It is crucial to remember that visa policies and criteria might change, therefore it is advised to check the U.S. Department of State's official website or speak with the closest U.S. embassy or consulate for the most recent information before making travel arrangements to Alaska.

CHAPTER 8

Health and Safety Tips

Vaccinations and Medical Preparations

Vaccinations and medical preparations for visitors to Alaska are essential to ensure a safe and healthy trip. Alaska is a vast and diverse state with unique environmental conditions, wildlife, and potential health risks. Therefore, it is important for visitors to be aware of the necessary vaccinations and medical precautions before traveling to this beautiful destination.

Vaccinations:

Before visiting Alaska, it is recommended that travelers ensure they are up to date on routine vaccinations such as measles-mumps-rubella (MMR), diphtheria-tetanus-pertussis (DTaP), varicella (chickenpox), polio, and influenza. These vaccines protect against common diseases that can be encountered anywhere in the world.

Additionally, there are specific vaccinations that may be recommended based on the traveler's individual circumstances and planned activities in Alaska. Some of these include:

- Hepatitis A: Hepatitis A is a viral infection that can be transmitted through contaminated food or water. It is recommended for all travelers to Alaska, as there may be instances where proper sanitation practices are not followed.

- Hepatitis B: Hepatitis B is a viral infection that can be transmitted through contact with infected blood or bodily fluids. It is recommended for travelers who may have intimate contact with locals or engage in activities that could lead to exposure, such as getting tattoos or piercings.
- Rabies: Rabies is a viral disease that can be transmitted through the bite or scratch of an infected animal. While the risk of rabies in Alaska is low, it is still advisable for travelers who plan to engage in outdoor activities or come into close contact with wildlife.
- Typhoid: Typhoid fever is a bacterial infection that can be contracted through contaminated food or water. It is recommended for travelers who will be staying in rural areas or eating at local establishments where hygiene standards may vary.
- Meningococcal: Meningococcal disease is a bacterial infection that can cause meningitis. It is recommended for travelers who will be in close contact with locals or participating in large gatherings or events.

- Tetanus: Tetanus is a bacterial infection that can enter the body through cuts or wounds. It is recommended for all travelers, as accidents can happen anywhere.

It is important to consult with a healthcare provider or travel medicine specialist well in advance of your trip to Alaska to determine which vaccinations are necessary based on your individual health status, planned activities, and previous immunizations.

Medical Preparations:

In addition to vaccinations, there are several medical preparations that visitors should consider before traveling to Alaska:

- Travel Insurance: It is highly recommended to have travel insurance that covers medical expenses, emergency medical evacuation, and trip cancellation/interruption. This ensures that you are financially protected in case of unexpected medical emergencies or trip disruptions.
- Prescription Medications: If you take prescription medications regularly, ensure that you have an ample supply for the duration of your trip. It is also advisable to carry a copy of your prescriptions and a letter from your healthcare provider explaining the need for the medication.

- First Aid Kit: Pack a basic first aid kit containing items such as band-aids, antiseptic ointment, pain relievers, insect repellent, sunscreen, and any other personal medications or supplies you may require.
- Altitude Sickness: If you plan to visit high-altitude areas in Alaska, such as Denali National Park or Mount McKinley, it is important to be aware of the symptoms and risks associated with altitude sickness. Gradual acclimatization and staying hydrated can help prevent or alleviate symptoms.
- Motion Sickness: If you are prone to motion sickness and plan to take boat or plane trips while in Alaska, consider bringing motion sickness medication or other remedies to alleviate discomfort.
- Bear Safety: Alaska is known for its wildlife, including bears. It is important to educate yourself on bear safety protocols and carry bear deterrents such as bear spray when venturing into bear country.

Keep in mind that these suggestions are only general advice, and that specific situations may differ. It is always best to consult with a healthcare professional or travel medicine specialist for personalized advice based on your specific needs and medical history.

Wildlife Safety Guidelines

Alaska is renowned for its diverse and abundant wildlife, including bears, moose, wolves, and marine mammals. While observing wildlife can be an exciting and memorable experience, it is crucial to prioritize safety for both visitors and the animals themselves. This comprehensive guide will provide wildlife safety guidelines for visitors to Alaska, ensuring a safe and enjoyable encounter with the state's remarkable wildlife.

General Wildlife Safety Guidelines:

- Maintain a Safe Distance: It is essential to keep a safe distance from all wildlife species encountered in Alaska. Approaching or attempting to touch wild animals can be dangerous and may provoke defensive behavior.
- Use Binoculars or Telephoto Lenses: To observe wildlife up close without disturbing them, use binoculars or telephoto lenses. This allows for a detailed view while maintaining a safe distance.
- Do Not Feed Wildlife: Feeding wildlife disrupts their natural behavior and can lead to dependency on human food sources. It also increases the risk of aggressive encounters.
- Secure Food and Garbage: When camping or picnicking in areas frequented by wildlife, store food and garbage

securely in bear-resistant containers or hang them from trees out of reach.
- **Respect Wildlife Closures:** Pay attention to any posted signs or closures indicating areas where wildlife is present or nesting. These closures are in place to protect both visitors and the animals.
- **Keep Pets Under Control:** If traveling with pets, ensure they are leashed at all times. Uncontrolled pets can disturb wildlife, provoke defensive behavior, or become targets for predators.

Bear Safety Guidelines:

- Make Noise: Bears have excellent hearing and will often avoid humans if they are aware of their presence. Make noise while hiking by talking, singing, or clapping hands to alert bears of your presence.
- Carry Bear Spray: When used correctly, bear spray is an extremely effective deterrent. Familiarize yourself with its proper use and carry it in an easily accessible location, such as a belt holster.
- Keep Calm and Back Away: If you come across a bear, keep calm and avoid making sudden moves. Back away slowly while facing the bear, giving it ample space to retreat.

- Do Not Run: Running may trigger a bear's predatory instinct. Avoid running, as it can provoke a chase response. Instead, maintain a slow and steady pace while moving away from the bear.
- Play Dead (If Attacked): In the rare event of a bear attack, playing dead is often the best strategy. To make it more difficult for the bear to flip you over, lie flat on your stomach with your hands clasped behind your neck and your legs spread apart.

Moose Safety Guidelines:

- Give Moose Space: Moose can be unpredictable and may become aggressive if they feel threatened. Maintain a safe distance of at least 50 feet (15 meters) from moose encountered in the wild.
- Watch for Signs of Aggression: If a moose displays signs of aggression, such as raised hackles, lowered head, or ears laid back, back away slowly and put a large object (like a tree or vehicle) between you and the moose.
- Do Not Approach Calves: Mother Moose are highly protective of their calves. Never approach or attempt to touch moose calves, as this can provoke an aggressive response from the mother.

- Be Cautious While Driving: Moose are frequently seen near roadways in Alaska. Exercise caution while driving, especially during dawn and dusk when moose are more active.

Marine Wildlife Safety Guidelines:

- Keep Your Distance: When observing marine wildlife such as whales, seals, or sea lions, maintain a safe distance of at least 100 yards (91 meters). Approaching too closely can disrupt their natural behavior and cause stress.
- Avoid Sudden Movements: Sudden movements or loud noises can startle marine wildlife and may cause them to react defensively. Move slowly and quietly to avoid disturbing them.
- Do Not Feed or Harass Marine Wildlife: Feeding marine wildlife is illegal and can harm their health. Additionally, avoid any actions that may harass or disturb these animals, such as chasing or surrounding them with boats.

By following these wildlife safety guidelines, visitors to Alaska can enjoy the incredible wildlife while minimizing risks to themselves and the animals. Remember, respecting wildlife and their habitats is crucial for their conservation and the preservation of Alaska's natural heritage.

Emergency Services

Emergency services in Alaska for visitors are essential to ensure the safety and well-being of individuals who may encounter unexpected situations or emergencies during their visit. Alaska, being a vast and remote state with diverse landscapes and challenging weather conditions, requires a robust emergency response system to cater to the needs of both residents and visitors.

Emergency Medical Services (EMS):

One of the primary emergency services available in Alaska is Emergency Medical Services (EMS). EMS provides pre-hospital medical care and transportation to individuals who require immediate medical attention. In Alaska, EMS is typically provided by local fire departments, private ambulance services, or community health centers. These services are equipped with trained paramedics and emergency medical technicians (EMTs) who can respond to various medical emergencies, including injuries, illnesses, and accidents.

In case of a medical emergency, visitors in Alaska should dial 911 to request assistance. The 911 emergency dispatchers will assess the situation and dispatch the appropriate EMS personnel to the location. It is important for visitors to provide accurate information about their location and the nature of the emergency to ensure a prompt response.

Search and Rescue (SAR):

Alaska's vast wilderness and rugged terrain make it a popular destination for outdoor activities such as hiking, camping, fishing, and wildlife viewing. However, these activities also come with inherent risks, and visitors may find themselves in need of search and rescue services.

The Alaska State Troopers coordinate search and rescue operations throughout the state. They work closely with local law enforcement agencies, volunteer organizations such as Alaska Mountain Rescue Group and Civil Air Patrol, as well as the U.S. Coast Guard for maritime incidents. Visitors who find themselves lost, injured, or stranded in remote areas should contact the Alaska State Troopers at their non-emergency number: 907-269-5511.

It is crucial for visitors engaging in outdoor activities to be well-prepared by carrying essential supplies such as maps, compasses, extra food and water, appropriate clothing, and communication devices. Additionally, informing someone about the planned activities and expected return time can aid in expediting search and rescue efforts if necessary.

Emergency Management Agencies:

Emergency management agencies play a vital role in coordinating emergency response efforts and providing information to the public during emergencies or natural disasters. In Alaska, the Division of Homeland Security and Emergency Management (DHSEM) is responsible for managing emergencies at the state level. DHSEM works closely with local emergency management agencies to ensure a coordinated response to emergencies.

The DHSEM provides various resources and information to help visitors prepare for emergencies while in Alaska. Their website offers guidance on creating emergency plans, assembling emergency supply kits, and staying informed about potential hazards. Visitors can access this information at www.ready.alaska.gov.

Additionally, the Federal Emergency Management Agency (FEMA) provides assistance during major disasters or emergencies that overwhelm local resources. FEMA works in collaboration with state and local agencies to provide support and resources to affected areas.

In conclusion, emergency services in Alaska for visitors encompass a range of essential services such as emergency medical services, search and rescue operations, and emergency management agencies. Visitors should be aware of the appropriate contact numbers for each service and take necessary precautions when engaging in outdoor activities. Being prepared and informed can help ensure a safe and enjoyable visit to Alaska.

CHAPTER 9

Packing Essentials

Clothing and Gear Recommendations

When packing clothing and gear for a trip to Alaska, it is important to consider the unique climate and outdoor activities that the state offers. Alaska is known for its diverse landscapes, ranging from icy glaciers to dense forests, and its weather can be unpredictable. Therefore, it is crucial to pack appropriately to ensure comfort and safety during your visit.

Clothing Recommendations:

Layering is key when it comes to dressing for Alaska's variable weather conditions. Consider the following important apparel items:

- Base Layers: Start with a good set of base layers made of moisture-wicking material such as merino wool or synthetic fabrics. These will help regulate body temperature and keep you dry.
- Insulating Layers: Pack insulating layers like fleece jackets or down vests to provide warmth in colder temperatures. These can be worn over base layers or under outer shells.

- Outer Shells: Invest in a waterproof and windproof jacket and pants to protect yourself from rain, snow, and strong winds. Look for garments with breathable membranes like Gore-Tex for optimal comfort.
- Pants: Opt for durable pants that are comfortable for outdoor activities such as hiking or exploring. Convertible pants that can be zipped off into shorts are also practical for varying temperatures.
- Footwear: Bring sturdy, waterproof hiking boots with good traction for exploring Alaska's trails and rugged terrain. Additionally, pack a pair of comfortable walking shoes or sneakers for everyday use.
- Socks: Pack several pairs of moisture-wicking socks made of wool or synthetic materials to keep your feet dry and warm. It's advisable to bring both thick and thin options for different weather conditions.
- Gloves, Hats, and Scarves: Don't forget to pack gloves, hats, and scarves to protect your extremities from the cold. Look for insulated options that provide adequate warmth.
- Swimwear: If you plan to visit Alaska during the summer months, consider packing swimwear for activities like kayaking, fishing, or visiting hot springs.

Gear Recommendations:

In addition to clothing, certain gear items are essential for a trip to Alaska. Here are some recommendations:

- Backpack: Bring a sturdy backpack to carry your essentials during outdoor activities. Look for one with comfortable straps and multiple compartments for organization.
- Daypack: Consider bringing a smaller daypack for shorter hikes or excursions. This will allow you to carry water, snacks, and other necessities without the bulk of a larger backpack.
- Binoculars: Alaska is known for its wildlife, so having a pair of binoculars can enhance your experience by allowing you to observe animals from a distance.
- Water Bottle: Stay hydrated by carrying a reusable water bottle with you. It's important to drink plenty of water, especially during physical activities and in dry climates.
- Headlamp/Flashlight: A headlamp or flashlight is essential for navigating in low-light conditions or during nighttime activities such as camping or hiking.
- Insect Repellent: Depending on the time of year and location within Alaska, mosquitoes and other insects can be prevalent. Pack insect repellant to keep bites at bay.

- Sun Protection: Even though Alaska is known for its cold climate, the sun can still be intense, especially during the summer months. To protect oneself from UV rays, bring sunscreen, sunglasses, and a hat.
- Camera and Accessories: Capture the stunning landscapes and wildlife encounters by bringing a camera with extra batteries and memory cards. Consider investing in a waterproof case or bag if you plan on engaging in water-based activities.
- First Aid Kit: It's always wise to have a basic first aid kit on hand for any minor injuries or ailments that may occur during your trip.
- Maps and Guidebooks: While technology can be helpful, it's a good idea to have physical maps and guidebooks as backup in case of limited connectivity or battery issues.

Remember to pack according to the specific activities you plan to engage in and the duration of your trip. It's also advisable to check the weather forecast before your departure and make any necessary adjustments to your packing list.

Essential Documents and Money

When traveling to Alaska as a visitor, it is crucial to pack essential documents and money to ensure a smooth and hassle-free trip. Proper preparation and organization of these items will help you navigate through various situations and emergencies that may arise during your visit. This comprehensive guide will outline the essential documents and money you should pack when traveling to Alaska.

Identification Documents:

One of the most important things to pack when visiting Alaska is identification documents. These documents are necessary for various purposes, including airport security checks, hotel check-ins, car rentals, and age verification for purchasing alcohol or entering certain establishments. Here are the identification documents you should consider bringing:

- Passport: If you are an international visitor, carrying your passport is mandatory. Ensure that your passport is valid for at least six months beyond your intended stay in Alaska.
- State ID or Driver's License: If you are a U.S. citizen, having a valid driver's license or state ID is essential. It can serve as an alternative form of identification if you prefer not to carry your passport at all times.
- Travel Visa: Depending on your country of origin, you may need a travel visa to enter the United States. Make sure to check the visa requirements well in advance and apply accordingly.

Travel Insurance Documents:

While it is not mandatory to have travel insurance when visiting Alaska, it is highly recommended. Travel insurance provides coverage for medical emergencies, trip cancellations or interruptions, lost baggage, and other unforeseen circumstances. When packing your travel insurance documents, consider the following:

- Insurance Policy Details: Carry a printed copy or digital version of your travel insurance policy that includes contact information for the insurance provider and policy number.
- Emergency Assistance Contact Information: Keep a separate note with emergency assistance contact numbers provided by your travel insurance company.

Financial Documents:

Managing your finances effectively during your trip to Alaska is crucial. Here are the essential financial documents you should pack:

- Credit and Debit Cards: Carry at least two credit or debit cards from different issuers to ensure you have backup options in case of loss, theft, or card malfunctions. Notify your bank or credit card company about your travel plans to avoid any potential issues with card usage.

- Cash: While credit and debit cards are widely accepted in most places in Alaska, it is advisable to carry some cash for emergencies or situations where cards may not be accepted. Ensure that you have small bills for convenience.
- Traveler's Checks: Although traveler's checks are not as commonly used today, some visitors still prefer them as a secure form of payment. If you choose to carry traveler's checks, make sure to keep a record of the check numbers separately from the checks themselves.

Itinerary and Reservation Documents:

To stay organized during your trip, it is essential to have all your itinerary and reservation documents readily available. These include:

- Flight Tickets: Print out or save electronic copies of your flight tickets, including any connecting flights or layovers.
- Hotel Reservations: Keep a copy of your hotel reservations, including confirmation numbers and contact information.
- Car Rental Reservations: If you plan on renting a car, carry the necessary documents such as reservation details, driver's license, and proof of insurance.

Health and Medication Documents:

If you have any pre-existing medical conditions or require specific medications, it is important to pack the following documents:

- Prescription Medications: Carry an adequate supply of prescription medications for the duration of your trip. Keep them in their original container with visible labeling.
- Doctor's Note or Prescription: If you are carrying controlled substances or injectable medications, it is advisable to have a doctor's note or prescription explaining the need for these medications.

Miscellaneous Documents:

In addition to the essential documents mentioned above, consider packing the following miscellaneous items:

- Travel Guidebook or Maps: Having a travel guidebook or maps can be helpful for navigating Alaska's attractions and finding your way around.
- Emergency Contact List: Prepare a list of emergency contacts, including family members, friends, and the contact information of your country's embassy or consulate in the United States.
- Copy of Important Documents: Make copies of all essential documents mentioned above and keep them separately

from the originals. This includes passports, identification cards, travel insurance documents, and reservation confirmations.

When packing these essential documents, it is crucial to keep them safe and secure throughout your trip. Consider using a waterproof document organizer or a secure travel wallet to protect them from damage or loss.

In conclusion, packing essential documents and money is vital when visiting Alaska as a visitor. By ensuring you have the necessary identification documents, travel insurance documents, financial documents, itinerary and reservation documents, health and medication documents, and miscellaneous items, you will be well-prepared for any situation that may arise during your trip.

CHAPTER 10

Activities and Attractions

Outdoor Adventures (hiking, fishing, kayaking, etc.)

Alaska, also known as "The Last Frontier," is an outdoor enthusiast's dream. With its vast wilderness, stunning landscapes, and abundant wildlife, it offers a wide range of outdoor adventures for visitors to enjoy. From hiking and fishing to kayaking and wildlife viewing, Alaska has something to offer for everyone seeking an unforgettable outdoor experience.

Hiking in Alaska:

Alaska boasts numerous hiking trails that cater to all skill levels, from beginners to experienced hikers. The state's diverse terrain includes mountains, glaciers, forests, and coastal areas, providing a variety of hiking options.

Denali National Park is one of the top places for hikers in Alaska. Home to North America's highest peak, Denali (formerly known as Mount McKinley), the park offers breathtaking views and a chance to spot wildlife such as grizzly bears, moose, and caribou. The park features a network of well-maintained trails that allow visitors to explore its pristine wilderness.

Another notable hiking destination is the Chugach State Park near Anchorage. With over 280 miles of trails, this park offers opportunities for day hikes as well as multi-day backpacking trips. Visitors can enjoy panoramic views of glaciers, mountains, and fjords while immersing themselves in the beauty of the Alaskan wilderness.

For those seeking a more challenging adventure, the Harding Icefield Trail in Kenai Fjords National Park is a must-visit. This strenuous 8.2-mile trail rewards hikers with stunning views of the expansive icefield and surrounding glaciers.

Fishing in Alaska:

Alaska is renowned for its world-class fishing opportunities. The state's rivers, lakes, and coastal waters are teeming with various fish species, including salmon, trout, halibut, and Arctic char.

The Kenai River is one of Alaska's premier fishing destinations. Known for its abundance of salmon, particularly the prized king salmon, it attracts anglers from around the world. The river offers both guided and unguided fishing options, allowing visitors to experience the thrill of reeling in a trophy fish.

Another popular fishing spot is the Bristol Bay region, home to the largest sockeye salmon run in the world. Anglers can enjoy fly fishing in pristine rivers and streams while surrounded by breathtaking scenery.

For those interested in saltwater fishing, the coastal waters of Alaska provide excellent opportunities to catch halibut, rockfish, and other species. Charter fishing trips are available in various locations, including Seward, Homer, and Sitka, offering visitors a chance to experience deep-sea fishing adventures.

Kayaking in Alaska:

Alaska's vast coastline and numerous lakes make it an ideal destination for kayaking enthusiasts. Whether you prefer calm waters or more challenging sea kayaking expeditions, Alaska has it all.

The Inside Passage is a popular kayaking route that stretches along the southeastern coast of Alaska. Paddlers can explore sheltered bays, fjords, and remote islands while encountering marine wildlife such as whales, sea otters, and seals.

Prince William Sound is another kayaking paradise. With its stunning glaciers and rugged coastline, it offers a unique paddling experience. Visitors can paddle among icebergs and witness calving glaciers up close while enjoying the tranquility of this pristine wilderness.

For those seeking a more adventurous kayaking trip, the remote waters of Glacier Bay National Park provide an unparalleled experience. Paddlers can navigate through icy waters surrounded by towering glaciers and snow-capped mountains.

Other Outdoor Adventures:

In addition to hiking, fishing, and kayaking, Alaska offers a plethora of other outdoor activities for visitors to enjoy. These include:

- Wildlife Viewing: Alaska is home to an array of wildlife species such as bears, wolves, eagles, and whales. Visitors can embark on wildlife viewing tours or simply keep an eye out for these majestic creatures while exploring the wilderness.
- Glacier Tours: Alaska is famous for its glaciers, and visitors can take boat tours or helicopter rides to witness these massive ice formations up close. Popular glacier destinations include Glacier Bay National Park, Kenai Fjords National Park, and the Matanuska Glacier.
- Dog Sledding: Experience the thrill of dog sledding, a traditional mode of transportation in Alaska. Visitors can take dog sled rides and learn about the history and culture of mushing.

Wildlife Viewing Opportunities

Alaska is renowned for its vast and diverse wildlife, offering visitors unparalleled opportunities to observe and appreciate a wide range of species in their natural habitats. From majestic marine mammals to iconic land animals, Alaska's wilderness provides a unique and unforgettable experience for wildlife enthusiasts. This comprehensive guide will highlight some of the top wildlife viewing opportunities in Alaska for visitors.

Denali National Park and Preserve: Located in the heart of Alaska, Denali National Park and Preserve is a prime destination for wildlife viewing. Spanning over six million acres, this park is home to an abundance of wildlife, including grizzly bears, moose, caribou, wolves, Dall sheep, and more. The park offers various guided tours and shuttle buses that take visitors deep into the wilderness, providing excellent opportunities to spot these magnificent creatures. The Denali Park Road, stretching 92 miles into the park, is a popular route for wildlife viewing.

Kenai Fjords National Park: Situated on the Kenai Peninsula in southern Alaska, Kenai Fjords National Park offers breathtaking scenery and exceptional wildlife viewing opportunities. The park's coastal waters are teeming with marine life, including humpback whales, orcas, sea otters, seals, and sea lions. Visitors can embark on boat tours or kayak excursions to witness these incredible creatures up close. Additionally, the park is home to numerous bird species, such as puffins and bald eagles, making it a paradise for birdwatchers.

Katmai National Park and Preserve: Located on the Alaska Peninsula, Katmai National Park and Preserve is renowned for its population of brown bears. The park's Brooks River is particularly famous for its bear viewing opportunities. Every summer, thousands of salmon migrate up the river, attracting numerous bears who gather to feast on this abundant food source. Visitors can observe these bears from designated viewing platforms, ensuring a safe and unforgettable experience. Katmai National Park also offers opportunities to spot other wildlife, including moose, wolves, and marine mammals.

Arctic National Wildlife Refuge: For those seeking a truly remote and untouched wilderness experience, the Arctic National Wildlife Refuge (ANWR) is an ideal destination. Located in northeastern Alaska, ANWR is the largest national wildlife refuge in the United States. The refuge is home to a diverse range of wildlife, including polar bears, muskoxen, caribou herds, wolves, and numerous bird species. Visitors can explore ANWR through guided tours or backpacking expeditions, immersing themselves in the pristine Arctic landscape and observing its unique inhabitants.

Prince William Sound: Situated on the southern coast of Alaska, Prince William Sound offers exceptional opportunities for marine wildlife viewing. The sound is home to a rich variety of marine mammals, including humpback whales, orcas, sea otters, seals, and porpoises. Visitors can embark on boat tours or kayak excursions to navigate the sound's pristine waters and witness these magnificent creatures in their natural habitat. Additionally, Prince William Sound is a haven for birdwatchers, with numerous seabirds and shorebirds inhabiting the area.

Tongass National Forest: As the largest national forest in the United States, Tongass National Forest encompasses vast stretches of southeastern Alaska's coastal rainforest. This diverse ecosystem provides habitat for a wide array of wildlife species. Visitors to Tongass National Forest may encounter black bears, bald eagles, Sitka black-tailed deer, mountain goats, and various bird species. Hiking trails and guided tours offer opportunities for wildlife observation within this stunning forested landscape.

Kodiak Island: Located off the southern coast of mainland Alaska, Kodiak Island is renowned for its population of Kodiak brown bears, the largest subspecies of brown bear in the world. Visitors can join guided bear viewing tours to observe these impressive creatures in their natural habitat. Kodiak Island is also home to other wildlife, including bald eagles, sea otters, seals, and a variety of marine bird species. The island's rugged coastline and pristine wilderness make it an ideal destination for wildlife enthusiasts.

Chugach State Park: Situated near Anchorage, Chugach State Park offers visitors a convenient opportunity to experience Alaska's wildlife without venturing too far from urban areas. The park encompasses diverse habitats, ranging from mountains to coastal areas, providing habitat for a wide range of wildlife species. Visitors may encounter moose, black bears, Dall sheep, mountain goats, and various bird species while exploring the park's extensive trail system.

Yukon River: The Yukon River, stretching over 2,000 miles through Alaska, offers unique wildlife viewing opportunities. This iconic river is home to diverse fish species, attracting numerous bald eagles that gather along its banks. Visitors can witness these majestic birds in large numbers during the salmon spawning season. Additionally, the Yukon River provides habitat for other wildlife, including moose, beavers, and waterfowl.

Alaska Maritime National Wildlife Refuge: Spanning approximately 3.4 million acres along Alaska's coastline, the Alaska Maritime National Wildlife Refuge is a haven for marine wildlife. This refuge comprises numerous islands and coastal areas that provide critical nesting and feeding grounds for seabirds and marine mammals. Visitors can take boat tours or join guided excursions to witness the incredible diversity of wildlife in this remote and pristine environment.

In conclusion, Alaska offers unparalleled wildlife viewing opportunities for visitors. From its vast national parks to its remote wilderness areas and coastal regions, this state is teeming with diverse animal species in their natural habitats. Whether observing grizzly bears in Denali National Park, witnessing marine mammals in Kenai Fjords National Park, or exploring the Arctic wilderness in ANWR, visitors to Alaska are sure to be captivated by the abundance and beauty of its wildlife.

Cultural Experiences (museums, festivals, etc.)

Alaska, known as "The Last Frontier," is a state rich in cultural experiences for visitors. From museums to festivals, there are numerous opportunities to immerse oneself in the unique heritage and traditions of this vast and diverse region. Whether you are interested in indigenous cultures, contemporary art, or local festivities, Alaska offers a wide range of cultural experiences that are sure to captivate and educate visitors.

Museums:

Alaska is home to several exceptional museums that showcase the state's history, art, and culture. These museums provide a glimpse into Alaska's past and present, offering visitors a deeper understanding of the region's heritage.

Anchorage Museum: Located in downtown Anchorage, the Anchorage Museum is the largest museum in Alaska and one of the top cultural attractions in the state. The museum features a diverse collection of exhibits that explore Alaska's art, history, science, and indigenous cultures. Visitors can learn about the state's native peoples through displays of traditional artifacts and contemporary artwork. The museum also hosts temporary exhibitions that highlight various aspects of Alaskan culture.

Alaska Native Heritage Center: Situated on 26 acres in Anchorage, the Alaska Native Heritage Center provides an immersive experience into the rich traditions and customs of Alaska's indigenous peoples. Visitors can explore authentic Native dwellings, watch traditional dance performances, participate in craft demonstrations, and interact with Native artists and storytellers. The center aims to preserve and promote the diverse cultures of Alaska's native communities.

University of Alaska Museum of the North: Located on the University of Alaska Fairbanks campus, this museum is renowned for its comprehensive collection of natural history specimens and cultural artifacts. The museum showcases Alaska's geological wonders, wildlife, and indigenous cultures through engaging exhibits. Visitors can marvel at ancient fossils, learn about Alaska's diverse ecosystems, and gain insights into the traditions and lifestyles of its native inhabitants.

Festivals:

Alaska's festivals provide a vibrant and lively celebration of the state's cultural diversity. These events offer visitors an opportunity to experience traditional music, dance, food, and customs firsthand.

Fur Rendezvous: Held annually in Anchorage, Fur Rendezvous is one of Alaska's oldest winter festivals. This multi-day event features a variety of activities, including sled dog races, snow sculpting competitions, carnival rides, and live performances. Visitors can also enjoy local cuisine and browse through arts and crafts exhibits that showcase Alaskan talent.

Sitka Summer Music Festival: Taking place in the picturesque coastal town of Sitka, this festival brings together renowned musicians from around the world for a series of classical music concerts. The festival offers a unique opportunity to enjoy chamber music performances in intimate venues while surrounded by the stunning natural beauty of Sitka.

World Eskimo-Indian Olympics: Celebrating Alaska's indigenous cultures, the World Eskimo-Indian Olympics (WEIO) is an annual event held in Fairbanks. The games feature traditional athletic competitions such as blanket toss, seal hop, and ear pull. Visitors can witness these impressive displays of strength and agility while also experiencing Native dance performances and cultural exhibitions.

In conclusion, Alaska offers a plethora of cultural experiences for visitors to explore. From museums that delve into the state's history and indigenous cultures to festivals that celebrate its diverse traditions, there is something for everyone to enjoy. These cultural experiences not only entertain but also educate visitors about the unique heritage and customs that make Alaska such a captivating destination.

CHAPTER 11

Food and Dining Options

Local Cuisine and Seafood Specialties

Alaska is renowned for its diverse and unique local cuisine, particularly its seafood specialties. Visitors to Alaska have the opportunity to indulge in a wide range of delicious dishes that showcase the state's abundant seafood resources. From fresh salmon to succulent king crab, Alaska offers a culinary experience like no other. In this comprehensive guide, we will explore some of the top local cuisine and seafood specialties in Alaska, including their prices and locations.

Salmon: Salmon is undoubtedly one of the most iconic seafood delicacies in Alaska. The state is home to five species of salmon: king (chinook), sockeye (red), coho (silver), pink, and chum. Each species has its own distinct flavor and texture, making it a versatile ingredient in various dishes.

- Price range: Depending on the type of salmon, the location of the restaurant, and the technique of cooking, salmon dishes might range in price. The typical price range for a salmon meal at a mid-range restaurant is between $20 and $40.

- Locations: You can find excellent salmon dishes throughout Alaska, but some notable locations include Anchorage, Juneau, and Sitka. In Anchorage, popular restaurants like Simon & Seaforts and Orso offer delectable salmon options on their menus. In Juneau, Tracy's King Crab Shack is a must-visit spot for mouthwatering salmon dishes. Sitka is known for its fresh seafood, and Ludvig's Bistro is a fantastic place to savor locally caught salmon.

King Crab: Alaska king crab is highly sought after for its sweet and tender meat. Known for its large size and impressive claws, king crab is a true delicacy that should not be missed during your visit to Alaska.

- Price Range: King crab can be quite expensive due to its limited availability and high demand. Prices can range from $50 to $100 per pound, depending on the size and quality of the crab. A typical king crab dinner at a restaurant can cost anywhere from $80 to $150.
- Locations: The best places to enjoy king crab in Alaska include Anchorage, Kodiak, and Dutch Harbor. In Anchorage, the Crab Pot Seafood Market is a popular spot for fresh king crab legs. Kodiak Island is known for its abundant king crab population, and local restaurants like Henry's Great Alaskan Restaurant offer delectable king

crab dishes. Dutch Harbor, located in the Aleutian Islands, is famous for its commercial fishing industry, and you can find excellent king crab options at local seafood markets.

Halibut: Halibut is another prized seafood specialty in Alaska. Known for its delicate flavor and firm texture, halibut is a versatile fish that can be prepared in various ways, including grilling, baking, or frying.

- Price Range: The price of halibut can vary depending on the season and location. On average, expect to pay around $25 to $40 for a halibut entree at a mid-range restaurant.
- Locations: Some top locations to savor halibut in Alaska include Homer, Seward, and Valdez. Homer is often referred to as the "Halibut Fishing Capital of the World," and you can find numerous restaurants offering fresh halibut dishes. Seward is another popular destination for halibut fishing, and local eateries like Ray's Waterfront offer mouthwatering halibut options. Valdez is known for its pristine waters and excellent fishing opportunities, making it an ideal place to enjoy fresh halibut.

In addition to these three seafood specialties, Alaska also offers a wide range of other local cuisine options such as reindeer sausage, smoked salmon dip, and Alaskan king salmon burgers. Exploring local farmers' markets and seafood festivals can provide a unique opportunity to taste a variety of Alaska's culinary delights.

Dining Recommendations

When visiting Alaska, there are numerous dining options available that cater to a variety of tastes and budgets. From seafood specialties to international cuisines, Alaska offers a diverse culinary scene that showcases the region's unique flavors. Here are some dining recommendations in Alaska for visitors, along with their prices and locations:

Simon & Seaforts - Located in Anchorage, Simon & Seaforts is a popular seafood restaurant known for its stunning views of the city skyline and the surrounding mountains. The menu features a wide range of seafood dishes, including fresh Alaskan salmon, halibut, and king crab legs. Prices at Simon & Seaforts can vary depending on the dish, but expect to spend around $30 to $50 per person for a main course. The restaurant also offers a happy hour menu with discounted prices on appetizers and drinks.

The Sourdough Mining Company - Situated in Anchorage, The Sourdough Mining Company is a family-friendly restaurant that combines Alaskan history with delicious comfort food. The menu includes hearty dishes such as prime rib, burgers, and Alaskan seafood chowder. Prices at The Sourdough Mining Company are relatively affordable, with main courses ranging from $15 to $30 per person. The restaurant's rustic atmosphere and friendly service make it a popular choice among locals and tourists alike.

The Saltry Restaurant - Located in Halibut Cove, a small community accessible by boat or seaplane from Homer, The Saltry Restaurant offers a unique dining experience in a picturesque waterfront setting. Known for its fresh seafood and organic ingredients sourced from local farms, this restaurant focuses on sustainable and seasonal cuisine. Prices at The Saltry Restaurant can be higher compared to other establishments due to its remote location and high-quality ingredients. Expect to spend around $40 to $60 per person for a main course.

The Double Musky Inn - Situated in Girdwood, The Double Musky Inn is a renowned restaurant that specializes in Cajun and Creole cuisine. The menu features dishes like blackened prime rib, jambalaya, and crawfish etouffee. Prices at The Double Musky Inn are moderate, with main courses ranging from $20 to $40 per person. The restaurant's lively atmosphere and unique flavors make it a favorite among locals and visitors alike.

The Pump House Restaurant & Saloon - Located in Fairbanks, The Pump House Restaurant & Saloon is housed in a historic building that dates back to the early 1900s. The menu offers a mix of Alaskan specialties and classic American dishes, including grilled salmon, bison burgers, and prime rib. Prices at The Pump

House can vary, but expect to spend around $25 to $45 per person for a main course. Additionally, the restaurant offers a wide selection of craft beers and an extensive wine list.

The Hangar on the Wharf - Situated in Juneau, The Hangar on the Wharf is a waterfront restaurant known for its fresh seafood and panoramic views of the Gastineau Channel. The menu features Alaskan favorites such as fish and chips, crab cakes, and grilled halibut. Prices at The Hangar on the Wharf are reasonable, with main courses ranging from $15 to $30 per person. The restaurant also has a lively bar area where visitors can enjoy local beers and cocktails.

These are just a few dining recommendations in Alaska for visitors. It's important to note that prices mentioned above are approximate and can vary depending on factors such as seasonal availability and market fluctuations. Additionally, it's always recommended to check the official websites or contact the restaurants directly for the most up-to-date information on prices and reservations.

CHAPTER 12

Budgeting and Expenses

Cost Considerations for Alaska Travel

When planning a trip to Alaska, it is essential to consider the various costs associated with travel. Alaska is known for its stunning landscapes, unique wildlife, and adventurous activities, but it can also be an expensive destination due to its remote location and limited infrastructure. To help you budget and make informed decisions, here are some cost considerations to keep in mind:

Transportation Costs:

- Flights: The cost of airfare to Alaska can vary significantly depending on the time of year, departure city, and how far in advance you book. Generally, flying during the peak summer season (June to August) tends to be more expensive. It is advisable to compare prices from different airlines and consider booking well in advance to secure better deals.

- Cruise: Another popular way to reach Alaska is by taking a cruise ship. Cruise prices can vary based on the duration of the trip, cabin type, and amenities offered. Additionally,

- Car Rental: If you plan on exploring Alaska independently, renting a car might be necessary. Car rental costs can vary depending on the type of vehicle, rental duration, and insurance coverage. It is recommended to compare prices from different rental companies and consider any additional fees such as mileage restrictions or one-way drop-off charges.

Accommodation Costs:

- Hotels: The cost of hotels in Alaska can vary greatly depending on the location and level of luxury. Major cities like Anchorage and Fairbanks tend to have a wider range of accommodation options at different price points. In more remote areas or during peak tourist season, prices may be higher. Consider booking accommodations well in advance to secure availability and potentially lower rates.
- Lodges/Cabins: For a more unique experience, many travelers opt for lodges or cabins located in scenic areas such as national parks or along the coastline. These accommodations can range from rustic to luxurious and often offer breathtaking views. Prices will vary depending on the location, amenities, and level of exclusivity.

keep in mind that onboard expenses such as dining, drinks, and excursions may not be included in the initial price.

- Camping: Alaska is known for its vast wilderness, making camping a popular and cost-effective option for outdoor enthusiasts. Campsite fees are generally lower compared to hotels or lodges, but keep in mind that you will need to bring your own camping gear or rent it locally.

Food and Dining Costs:

- Restaurants: Dining out in Alaska can be quite expensive, especially in touristy areas. Prices for meals at restaurants will vary depending on the type of cuisine and location. To save money, consider exploring local markets and grocery stores for picnic supplies or cooking your own meals if you have access to kitchen facilities.
- Seafood: Alaska is renowned for its fresh seafood, including salmon, halibut, and king crab. While dining on seafood can be a highlight of your trip, it is important to note that prices for these delicacies can be higher compared to other types of cuisine.
- Alcohol: If you plan on enjoying alcoholic beverages during your trip, keep in mind that alcohol prices in Alaska tend to be higher due to taxes and transportation costs. Consider purchasing alcohol from duty-free shops at airports or bringing your own if allowed by airline regulations.

Activities and Excursions Costs:

- Tours: Alaska offers a wide range of tours and excursions, such as wildlife viewing, glacier hikes, dog sledding, and fishing trips. The cost of these activities will vary depending on the duration, level of exclusivity, and equipment provided. Research different tour operators and compare prices to find the best value for your interests.
- National Park Fees: If you plan on visiting any of Alaska's national parks, such as Denali National Park or Kenai Fjords National Park, be aware that there may be entrance fees. These fees contribute to the maintenance and preservation of the parks and can range from a few dollars to a higher amount for annual passes.
- Equipment Rental: Depending on the activities you plan to engage in, you may need to rent equipment such as hiking gear, fishing gear, or kayaks. Rental costs will vary depending on the duration and type of equipment needed.

Miscellaneous Costs:

- Travel Insurance: It is highly recommended to have travel insurance when visiting Alaska, as unexpected events or emergencies can occur. The cost of travel insurance will depend on factors such as your age, duration of travel, and coverage options.

- Souvenirs: If you enjoy collecting souvenirs or gifts, budgeting for these expenses is important. Prices for souvenirs can vary greatly depending on their uniqueness and quality.
- Tips and Gratuities: In Alaska, tipping is customary for services such as dining in restaurants, guided tours, and hotel staff. It is advisable to budget for tips as they are not always included in the initial price.

It is important to note that the amounts mentioned above are subject to change and can vary based on individual preferences, travel dates, and other factors. Researching current prices and comparing options from different sources will help you make more accurate estimations for your specific trip.

Money-Saving Tips

Traveling to Alaska can be an exciting and memorable experience, but it can also be quite expensive. From transportation to accommodation and activities, the costs can quickly add up. However, with careful planning and a few money-saving tips, you can make your Alaska travel more affordable without compromising on the quality of your trip. As a traveler with knowledge, I will provide you with some valuable tips to help you save money during your Alaska adventure.

- Plan your trip during the shoulder season: Alaska's peak tourist season is typically from June to August when the weather is warmer and wildlife is abundant. However, traveling during this time can be costly due to high demand. Consider visiting during the shoulder season, which is in May or September. During these months, you can still enjoy pleasant weather and witness breathtaking natural beauty while benefiting from lower prices on flights, accommodations, and tours.
- Be flexible with your travel dates: If you have the flexibility to choose your travel dates, consider searching for the best deals. Flight fares vary greatly based on the day of the week and the season. Use flight comparison websites or sign up for fare alerts to stay updated on any price drops or special promotions. Being flexible with your travel dates can help you secure cheaper flights to Alaska.
- Take advantage of local transportation options: While renting a car may seem like a convenient option for exploring Alaska, it can also be expensive due to high rental fees and fuel costs. Instead, consider utilizing local transportation options such as buses or shuttles. Many towns in Alaska have reliable public transportation systems

that can take you to popular attractions at a fraction of the cost. Additionally, some tour operators offer transportation services as part of their packages, which can be a more cost-effective way to visit multiple destinations.

- Cook your own meals: Dining out in Alaska can be pricey, especially in remote areas where restaurants are limited. To save money on food, consider booking accommodations with kitchen facilities or staying in vacation rentals. This will allow you to prepare your own meals using local ingredients, which can be a fun and budget-friendly way to experience the local cuisine. Additionally, shopping at local grocery stores instead of tourist-oriented shops can help you save even more.
- Research and book tours in advance: Alaska offers a wide range of outdoor activities and tours, from glacier hikes to wildlife cruises. To save money, research and book your tours in advance. Many tour operators offer early bird discounts or online promotions that can significantly reduce the cost of your activities. By planning ahead, you can also ensure availability for popular tours, as they tend to fill up quickly during peak season.
- Take advantage of free or low-cost attractions: Alaska is known for its stunning natural beauty, and there are plenty of free or low-cost attractions to explore. National parks

such as Denali and Kenai Fjords offer breathtaking landscapes and wildlife viewing opportunities at a minimal entrance fee. Additionally, many towns have museums, visitor centers, and cultural sites that offer free or discounted admission. Take advantage of these attractions to immerse yourself in Alaska's rich history and natural wonders without breaking the bank.

- Pack appropriately for the weather: Alaska's weather can be unpredictable, so it's essential to pack accordingly to avoid unnecessary expenses. Bring layers of clothing that can be easily added or removed depending on the temperature fluctuations. This will help you stay comfortable without having to purchase expensive gear on-site. Additionally, don't forget essentials like rain gear and sturdy footwear for outdoor activities.

- Consider alternative accommodation options: While hotels can be convenient, they are often more expensive than alternative accommodation options in Alaska. Consider staying in bed and breakfasts, hostels, or vacation rentals, which can provide a more affordable and authentic experience. These options often come with additional amenities such as kitchen facilities, allowing you to save money on meals.

- Look for local deals and discounts: Keep an eye out for local deals and discounts offered by businesses in Alaska. Many restaurants, shops, and tour operators provide special promotions or coupons that can help you save money. Check local tourism websites, visitor centers, or ask locals for recommendations on where to find the best deals.
- Travel with a group: If you're traveling with friends or family, consider exploring Alaska as a group. Group rates are often available for accommodations, tours, and transportation, allowing you to save money while enjoying shared experiences. Additionally, splitting costs for things like car rentals or vacation rentals can significantly reduce individual expenses.

By implementing these money-saving tips, you can make your Alaska travel more affordable without compromising on the quality of your experience. Remember to plan ahead, be flexible, and take advantage of local resources and deals. With careful budgeting and smart choices, you can enjoy all that Alaska has to offer while keeping your wallet happy.

CHAPTER 13

Communication and Connectivity

Mobile Networks and Internet Access

As a traveler with knowledge on mobile networks and internet access for Alaska travel, I can provide you with a comprehensive overview of the topic. Alaska, being the largest state in the United States, presents unique challenges when it comes to mobile networks and internet access due to its vast and remote landscape.

Mobile Networks in Alaska:

Alaska is known for its rugged terrain and sparse population, which makes it more challenging to provide comprehensive mobile network coverage across the state. However, major mobile network providers like AT&T, Verizon, T-Mobile, and GCI (General Communication Inc.) offer coverage in various parts of Alaska. These providers utilize a combination of technologies such as 4G LTE, 3G, and even satellite connections to ensure connectivity in remote areas.

It is important to note that while major cities like Anchorage, Fairbanks, and Juneau have relatively good mobile network coverage, more remote areas may have limited or no coverage at all. This is due to the vast distances between communities and the challenging terrain. Therefore, it is advisable to research the specific regions you plan to visit in Alaska to determine the availability of mobile network coverage.

Internet Access in Alaska:

Internet access in Alaska can vary significantly depending on your location. In urban areas like Anchorage and Fairbanks, you can expect reliable high-speed internet connections similar to other major cities in the United States. These areas are well-served by cable and fiber optic networks.

However, as you venture into more remote parts of Alaska, internet access becomes less reliable and slower. Many rural communities rely on satellite internet connections due to the lack of terrestrial infrastructure. While satellite internet can provide connectivity in these areas, it often comes with limitations such as higher latency and data usage restrictions.

In some cases, certain lodges or accommodations in remote areas may offer limited internet access through Wi-Fi hotspots or satellite connections. However, it is important to manage your expectations and be prepared for slower speeds and potential limitations on data usage.

Tips for Mobile Networks and Internet Access in Alaska:

- Research Coverage: Before your trip to Alaska, research the coverage maps of different mobile network providers to determine which one offers the best coverage in the regions you plan to visit. This will help you choose a provider that suits your needs.//
- Consider Multiple Providers: Due to variations in coverage, it may be beneficial to have SIM cards from multiple mobile network providers. This way, if one provider has limited coverage in a particular area, you can switch to another provider for better connectivity.
- Offline Maps and Apps: In areas with limited or no internet access, it is advisable to download offline maps and travel apps that can be accessed without an internet connection. This will help you navigate and find information even when you are offline.
- Satellite Communication: If you are traveling to extremely remote areas where mobile network coverage is unlikely, consider investing in satellite communication devices such as satellite phones or satellite messengers. These devices can provide a reliable means of communication in emergency situations.
- Plan for Limited Connectivity: Embrace the opportunity to disconnect from the digital world and enjoy the natural

beauty of Alaska. Plan activities that do not rely heavily on internet access and take advantage of the stunning landscapes and wildlife that Alaska has to offer.

In conclusion, mobile networks and internet access in Alaska can vary depending on your location. While major cities have reliable coverage, more remote areas may have limited or no connectivity. It is important to research coverage maps, consider multiple providers, and plan for limited connectivity when traveling in Alaska.

Communication Tips for Remote Areas

As a traveler with knowledge of remote areas in Alaska, I can provide you with some communication tips to ensure a smooth and safe journey. Alaska is known for its vast wilderness and remote locations, which can present challenges when it comes to staying connected. However, with the right preparation and equipment, you can maintain communication even in the most isolated areas.

Research and Plan Ahead:

Before embarking on your trip to remote areas in Alaska, it is crucial to conduct thorough research and plan ahead for your communication needs. Familiarize yourself with the specific region you will be visiting and gather information about the available communication options in that area. This will help you determine the best approach to stay connected during your travels.

Satellite Phones:

In remote areas where traditional cellular networks are unavailable or unreliable, satellite phones are an excellent option for maintaining communication. These phones use satellites orbiting the Earth to establish connections, allowing you to make calls, send text messages, and even access basic internet services. It is advisable to rent or purchase a satellite phone before your trip and ensure that you are familiar with its operation.

Two-Way Radios:

Two-way radios, also known as walkie-talkies, are another useful tool for communication in remote areas of Alaska. They operate on specific radio frequencies and do not rely on cellular networks or satellite connections. Two-way radios are particularly beneficial when traveling in groups or when exploring areas with limited cell coverage. Make sure to bring extra batteries and test the range of your radios before setting out on your journey.

Personal Locator Beacons (PLBs):

Personal Locator Beacons (PLBs) are compact devices that can be a lifesaver in emergency situations. These devices use satellite technology to transmit distress signals to search and rescue authorities, enabling them to locate you quickly. PLBs should be registered with the appropriate authorities before your trip, and it is essential to understand how to activate and use them effectively.

Offline Maps and GPS Devices:

In remote areas where internet connectivity may be limited or nonexistent, having offline maps and a reliable GPS device is crucial. Before your trip, download offline maps of the areas you plan to visit on your smartphone or tablet. Additionally, consider investing in a dedicated GPS device that can function without an internet connection. These tools will help you navigate and stay on track even when you are off the grid.

Emergency Contact Information:

Always carry a list of emergency contact numbers specific to the region you are traveling in. This should include local authorities, search and rescue services, medical facilities, and any other relevant emergency contacts. In case of an emergency, having this information readily available can save valuable time and potentially be life-saving.

Weather Updates:

Weather conditions in remote areas can change rapidly, so it is essential to stay informed about any potential storms or severe weather events. Check local weather forecasts regularly before and during your trip. NOAA Weather Radio is a reliable source for up-to-date weather information in Alaska's remote regions.

Satellite Internet Services:

If you require more extensive communication capabilities, such as accessing emails or browsing the internet, satellite internet services may be an option worth considering. These services utilize satellite connections to provide internet access even in remote areas. They are, however, costly and may necessitate specialist equipment.

Local Knowledge and Advice:

When traveling to remote areas in Alaska, it is always beneficial to seek advice from locals or experienced travelers who have been to the same region before. They can provide valuable insights into the specific communication challenges you may encounter and offer tips based on their firsthand experiences.

Remember that communication in remote areas of Alaska can be unpredictable, and it is essential to have backup plans in place. Always inform someone about your travel plans, including your expected itinerary and return date. Regularly check in with a trusted contact to ensure your safety and provide updates on your progress.

In conclusion, staying connected in remote areas of Alaska requires careful planning and the right equipment. Researching communication options, carrying satellite phones or two-way radios, having a PLB, using offline maps and GPS devices, and staying informed about weather conditions are all essential steps to ensure effective communication during your travels.

CHAPTER 14

Travel Insurance

Importance of Travel Insurance

As a traveler with knowledge, I can confidently state that having travel insurance is of utmost importance when planning a trip to Alaska. Alaska is a unique and beautiful destination known for its stunning landscapes, wildlife, and outdoor activities. However, it also presents certain risks and challenges that make travel insurance an essential aspect of any trip to this region.

One of the primary reasons why travel insurance is crucial for Alaska travel is the remote and rugged nature of the state. Alaska is vast and largely undeveloped, with many areas inaccessible by road. This means that travelers often rely on small aircraft, boats, or other unconventional modes of transportation to reach their destinations. While these methods can provide incredible experiences, they also come with inherent risks. Inclement weather conditions, mechanical failures, or other unforeseen circumstances can lead to delays, cancellations, or even accidents. Having travel insurance ensures that you are financially protected in such situations and can receive assistance or compensation for any losses incurred.

Another significant factor to consider is the potential for medical emergencies during your trip to Alaska. The state's remote locations and limited healthcare facilities can pose challenges in case of illness or injury. In some cases, medical evacuation may be necessary to transport you to a more advanced medical facility. Travel insurance can cover the costs associated with emergency medical treatment, evacuation, and repatriation if needed. This coverage provides peace of mind knowing that you will receive appropriate care without incurring exorbitant expenses.

Additionally, Alaska's unpredictable weather patterns and harsh environment make it susceptible to natural disasters such as earthquakes, avalanches, or severe storms. These events can disrupt travel plans and cause significant inconvenience or even danger to travelers. Travel insurance can protect you from trip cancellations or disruptions caused by unanticipated events beyond your control. It can also provide coverage for additional expenses incurred due to delays or alternative arrangements needed as a result of such events.

Furthermore, Alaska is home to a diverse range of wildlife, including bears, moose, and other potentially dangerous animals. While encounters with wildlife can be thrilling, they also carry certain risks. Travel insurance can provide coverage for medical expenses resulting from animal attacks or accidents caused by encounters with wildlife.

In summary, travel insurance is essential for Alaska travel due to the remote and rugged nature of the state, the potential for medical emergencies in remote areas, the risk of natural disasters, and the possibility of encounters with wildlife. It offers financial protection and peace of mind, ensuring that you can enjoy your trip without worrying about unforeseen circumstances or unexpected expenses.

Coverage Options

Travel insurance is an essential aspect of planning any trip, especially when traveling to a destination like Alaska. The vast wilderness, extreme weather conditions, and remote locations make it crucial to have adequate coverage in case of unforeseen circumstances. In this comprehensive guide, we will explore the coverage options available for travel insurance specifically tailored for Alaska travel.

Trip Cancellation and Interruption Coverage: One of the primary coverage options offered by travel insurance is trip cancellation and interruption coverage. This type of coverage protects you financially if you need to cancel or cut short your trip due to covered reasons such as illness, injury, or death of a family member. It often reimburses you for non-refundable charges such as airfare, lodging, and tour reservations.

Emergency Medical Coverage: Another crucial aspect of travel insurance for Alaska travel is emergency medical coverage. Alaska's remote locations and rugged terrain can pose risks for accidents or medical emergencies. Emergency medical coverage provides financial protection for medical expenses incurred during your trip, including hospital stays, doctor visits, prescription medications, and emergency medical evacuations if necessary.

Baggage and Personal Belongings Coverage: Baggage and personal belongings coverage is designed to protect your belongings against loss, theft, or damage during your trip. In Alaska's wilderness, where outdoor activities like hiking and camping are popular, there is a higher risk of losing or damaging your belongings. This coverage typically reimburses you for the cost of replacing lost or damaged items such as luggage, electronics, cameras, and sporting equipment.

Travel Delay Coverage: Alaska's unpredictable weather conditions can lead to flight delays or cancellations. Travel delay coverage provides reimbursement for additional expenses incurred due to unexpected delays, such as accommodation costs, meals, and transportation.

Emergency Evacuation Coverage: Alaska's remote areas may require emergency evacuation in case of natural disasters, accidents, or medical emergencies. Emergency evacuation coverage ensures that you are financially protected if you need to be transported to the nearest medical facility or evacuated from a dangerous situation.

Adventure Activities Coverage: Alaska offers a wide range of adventure activities like hiking, kayaking, fishing, and wildlife viewing. If you plan to participate in these activities, it is essential to check if your travel insurance covers them. Some policies may exclude coverage for certain high-risk activities, so make sure to read the policy details carefully.

24/7 Assistance Services: Many travel insurance providers offer 24/7 assistance services that can be invaluable during emergencies. These services often include access to a helpline for medical advice, assistance with finding local medical facilities, and help with travel arrangements in case of trip disruptions.

It is important to note that coverage options and policy terms may vary among different travel insurance providers. It is recommended to carefully review the policy documents and understand the coverage limits, exclusions, and claim procedures before purchasing travel insurance for your Alaska trip.

CHAPTER 15

Responsible Travel Practices

Environmental Conservation

Environmental conservation for Alaska travel is a crucial aspect that needs to be considered in order to preserve the natural beauty and ecological balance of this unique destination. Alaska is known for its stunning landscapes, diverse wildlife, and pristine wilderness, making it a popular choice for travelers seeking an immersive and authentic outdoor experience. However, the increasing number of visitors to Alaska has raised concerns about the potential negative impacts on the environment. Therefore, it is essential to promote sustainable practices and responsible tourism to ensure the long-term preservation of Alaska's natural resources.

One of the key areas of focus for environmental conservation in Alaska travel is minimizing the carbon footprint associated with transportation. Traveling to Alaska often involves long-haul flights or cruises, which contribute significantly to greenhouse gas emissions. To address this issue, it is important to encourage travelers to choose more sustainable transportation options whenever possible. This can include opting for direct flights, using fuel-efficient vehicles for local transportation, or even considering alternative modes of travel such as train or bus.

Another critical aspect of environmental conservation in Alaska travel is the protection of wildlife and their habitats. Alaska is home to a wide range of iconic species, including bears, moose, wolves, whales, and numerous bird species. It is essential to respect wildlife and their natural habitats by adhering to guidelines and regulations set by local authorities and conservation organizations. This includes maintaining a safe distance from animals, not feeding them, and avoiding any activities that may disrupt their natural behavior or breeding patterns.

Furthermore, waste management plays a significant role in environmental conservation efforts in Alaska. With the increasing number of tourists visiting remote areas, proper waste disposal becomes crucial to prevent pollution and preserve the pristine environment. Travelers should be encouraged to follow the principles of "leave no trace" by packing out all their trash and disposing of it properly in designated areas. Additionally, promoting the use of reusable water bottles and reducing single-use plastics can help minimize waste generation.

Preserving Alaska's fragile ecosystems also involves supporting local conservation initiatives and sustainable tourism practices. Travelers can contribute to environmental conservation by choosing tour operators and accommodations that prioritize sustainability. This can include staying in eco-friendly lodges or participating in guided tours that promote responsible wildlife viewing and outdoor activities. By supporting local businesses that prioritize environmental stewardship, travelers can contribute to the long-term preservation of Alaska's natural resources.

In conclusion, environmental conservation for Alaska travel is of utmost importance to ensure the preservation of its unique ecosystems and wildlife. By promoting sustainable transportation, respecting wildlife and their habitats, practicing proper waste management, and supporting local conservation initiatives, travelers can play a significant role in preserving the natural beauty of Alaska for future generations.

Respect for Local Communities

Respect for local communities in Alaska travel is a crucial aspect that should be prioritized by both travelers and the tourism industry. Alaska is home to diverse indigenous communities, each with its unique culture, traditions, and way of life. It is essential to approach travel in Alaska with respect, sensitivity, and a commitment to preserving the local communities' well-being and cultural heritage.

One of the fundamental principles of respecting local communities in Alaska travel is acknowledging and honoring their sovereignty and self-determination. Many indigenous communities in Alaska have a long history of resilience and have fought hard to maintain their cultural identity and rights. Recognizing their sovereignty means understanding that they have the right to control their lands, resources, and cultural practices.

When visiting Alaska, it is important to engage with local communities in a respectful manner. This includes seeking permission before entering their lands or participating in any cultural activities or events. Many indigenous communities offer opportunities for visitors to learn about their traditions, such as storytelling, dance performances, or craft demonstrations. It is crucial to approach these experiences with an open mind, showing appreciation for the knowledge shared and refraining from appropriating or commodifying their culture.

Respecting local communities also involves supporting their economic development and sustainability. When choosing accommodations, dining options, or tour operators, consider those that are owned and operated by local community members. This helps ensure that the economic benefits of tourism are distributed more equitably among the local population. Additionally, purchasing locally made crafts or products directly from artisans provides them with a source of income and helps preserve traditional craftsmanship.

Environmental stewardship is another important aspect of respecting local communities in Alaska travel. The state's pristine natural landscapes are not only breathtaking but also hold immense cultural significance for indigenous communities. It is crucial to follow Leave No Trace principles when exploring these areas, minimizing our impact on the environment and respecting wildlife habitats. Additionally, being mindful of local regulations regarding hunting, fishing, or gathering resources is essential to preserve the delicate balance of Alaska's ecosystems.

Education and awareness play a vital role in fostering respect for local communities in Alaska travel. Taking the time to learn about the history, traditions, and challenges faced by indigenous communities can help visitors develop a deeper understanding and appreciation for their culture. This knowledge can also help travelers avoid unintentional cultural insensitivity or offensive behavior.

In conclusion, respecting local communities in Alaska travel is not only a matter of ethical responsibility but also an enriching experience for travelers. By acknowledging indigenous sovereignty, engaging respectfully, supporting local economies, practicing environmental stewardship, and educating ourselves, we can contribute to the preservation and celebration of Alaska's diverse cultures.

CHAPTERT 16

Conclusion

Alaska, the largest state in the United States, is a land of breathtaking natural beauty and unique experiences. As a guest visiting this remarkable destination, you will be captivated by its stunning landscapes, abundant wildlife, and rich cultural heritage. In this conclusion, we will summarize the key highlights of Alaska from a visitor's perspective.

First and foremost, Alaska is renowned for its majestic wilderness. The state is home to numerous national parks and preserves, including Denali National Park and Preserve, Glacier Bay National Park and Preserve, and Kenai Fjords National Park. These protected areas offer unparalleled opportunities for outdoor enthusiasts to explore pristine forests, towering mountains, massive glaciers, and diverse ecosystems. Whether you choose to hike through the rugged terrain, embark on a thrilling wildlife safari, or simply soak in the awe-inspiring scenery, Alaska's wilderness will leave an indelible mark on your soul.

In addition to its natural wonders, Alaska boasts a vibrant wildlife population. From grizzly bears and moose to bald eagles and humpback whales, the state is teeming with fascinating creatures. Imagine witnessing a pod of orcas breaching the surface of the ocean or observing brown bears catching salmon in their powerful jaws. These encounters with wildlife are not only awe-inspiring but also serve as a reminder of the delicate balance of nature.

Furthermore, Alaska offers a glimpse into its rich cultural heritage. The state is home to several indigenous communities that have inhabited these lands for thousands of years. By engaging with local tribes and participating in cultural activities such as traditional dances and storytelling sessions, visitors can gain a deeper understanding of Alaska's native peoples and their enduring traditions. Additionally, museums and heritage centers provide valuable insights into the history and artistry of these communities.

As a guest in Alaska, you will also have the opportunity to partake in various outdoor activities. Fishing enthusiasts can cast their lines in pristine rivers and lakes, hoping to catch salmon, trout, or halibut. Adventure seekers can embark on thrilling dog sledding expeditions or go kayaking amidst towering icebergs. For those seeking a more relaxed experience, scenic cruises along the Inside Passage offer breathtaking views of fjords, glaciers, and coastal wildlife.

Lastly, Alaska's unique geographical location provides visitors with the chance to witness extraordinary natural phenomena. The state is renowned for its midnight sun during the summer months when the sun remains visible for almost 24 hours a day. In contrast, the winter months offer the opportunity to witness the mesmerizing Northern Lights dancing across the night sky.

In conclusion, Alaska is a destination that offers an unparalleled experience for guests from all walks of life. Its majestic wilderness, abundant wildlife, rich cultural heritage, and diverse range of outdoor activities make it a truly remarkable place to visit. Whether you are seeking adventure, tranquility, or a deeper connection with nature and indigenous cultures, Alaska has something to offer everyone.

Safe Travel!

Made in United States
Troutdale, OR
11/25/2023

14889153R00086